Mount Analogue

Mount Analogue

A Novel of Symbolically Authentic Non-Euclidean Adventures in Mountain Climbing

RENÉ DAUMAL
TRANSLATION AND INTRODUCTION BY
Roger Shattuck

WITH A POSTFACE BY
Véra Daumal

TRANSLATED FROM THE DEFINITIVE EDITION
ESTABLISHED BY
H. J. Maxwell and C. Rugafiori

Shambhala
Boston
1986

SHAMBHALA PUBLICATIONS, INC.
314 DARTMOUTH STREET
BOSTON, MASSACHUSETTS 02116

9 8 7 6 5 4 3 2 1

FIRST SHAMBHALA EDITION
Published by arrangement with Pantheon Books, a division of Random House, Inc.
Printed in the United States of America
Distributed in the United States by Random House
and in Canada by Random House of Canada Ltd.

Library of Congress Cataloging-in-Publication Data
Daumal, René, 1908–1944.
Mount Analogue: a novel of symbolically authentic non-Euclidean adventures in mountain climbing.
Translation of: Le Mont Analogue.
I. Title.
PQ2607.A86M613 1986 843'.912 86-11843
ISBN 0-87773-381-3 (pbk.)

Contents

Translator's Note

René Daumal's works have been appearing at irregular intervals ever since his death in 1944, and his reputation as the voice of the spiritual and the pataphysical in literature has grown steadily and silently, like a cistern fed by underground springs.

Each volume reveals new ways in which he sought to reconcile the farthest fringes of European thought with his genuine knowledge of the occult, the Oriental and the spiritual. No fad or frivolity attaches to the integrity of his probings. His journey traversed some of the most exciting countries of the mind: experiments with induced states of consciousness, a sustained attempt to form a spiritual-artistic community in Paris, and deep philological and philosophical research into the universe of Sanskrit texts. Significantly, the first author he alludes to in the essay 'A Fundamental Experience' is William James, the no-nonsense philosopher-scientist of the mind whose writings on psychology and religion have not faded. Daumal's later works must be seen both in their relationship to James's acknowledgement of 'overbelief' and in their direct relationship to the teaching of Georges Gurdjieff.

Born in Armenia and trained primarily in Tibet, Gurdjieff was the Paris sage whose synthesis of Eastern and European thought had a powerful fascination for many writers and intellectuals in the West between the wars. His Paris community attracted such luminaries as Katherine Mansfield. One of Gurdjieff's French disciples, Alexandre de Salzmann, was close to Daumal and introduced him into the community, where Daumal attended a few classes in his final years while he was writing *Mount Analogue*. 'Father' Sogol, the organizer of the expedition, is modelled partially on Salzmann.

Yet Daumal had found his spiritual orientation well before encountering Gurdjieff.

The English translation of *Mount Analogue* has been brought out successively by five different publishers, with one attempted piracy along the way. Daumal's first novel, *La Grande Beuverie*, has been published in England and the United States under the title *A Night of Serious Drinking*.

In 1981 a 'definitive version' of *Mount Analogue* edited by H. J. Maxwell and C. Rugafiori was brought out in Paris by Éditions Gallimard. This new English edition follows the new French edition with the addition of the introduction and of the postface by Véra Daumal on pages 103 to 105. The 'definitive version' in French carries the following Editor's Foreword:

'René Daumal began *Mount Analogue* in July 1939 during his stay in Pelvoux in the Alps, a particularly tragic moment in his life. He had just learned – at the age of thirty-one – that he would not live long. The years of tuberculosis had undermined his health beyond cure. Daumal had finished three chapters by June 1940 when he left Paris because of the German occupation. His wife, Véra Milanova, was Jewish. After three years of terrible hardships in the Pyrenees (Gavarnie), in the Marseilles region (Allauch), and in the Alps (Passy, Pelvoux), Daumal had a period of remission in the summer of 1943 during which he hoped to complete his "novel". He began writing again, but the final relapse came while he was still working on Chapter 5. He died in Paris on 21 May 1944.

'Though the book remains unfinished, the structure of *Mount Analogue* articulates the single goal of Daumal's story. The reader can reconstitute the end of this "mountain tale" by referring to Daumal's outlines [pages 108 to 109] and to the texts [at the end of the edition] – particularly the summary . . . They make the end "transparent".'

ROGER SHATTUCK
Dakar, Senegal, 1985

Introduction

There are considerable portions of René Daumal's thinking that leave one with the sensation of watching a man climb out of sight on a steep slope. Yet there is no display of superiority or showmanship in his progress. Climbing was both his vocation and his avocation, and he simply kept on going when others turned back. It is not surprising that Daumal's fame as a writer commenced only after his death at the age of thirty-six.

Still in his teens during the late twenties, Daumal was already publishing avant-garde poetry, was training himself in Oriental languages, and at twenty helped found a lively literary review. He was associated for a time with the controversial Russian teacher and sage, Georges Gurdjieff; his own philosophical study kept him intent on comprehending and reaffirming the dialectical method of the West as complementary to the spiritual discipline of the East. To this end Daumal began by writing in every form except fiction. Yet, while still young, he knew it was time to fuse his understanding of life into a single work. At that point he began a novel. It makes no reference to esoteric knowledge; the events it narrates are incredible yet entirely plausible. The work remained unfinished when he died, but enough had been written to allow us to grasp the whole.

Mount Analogue, as he called that novel, speaks for itself. An introduction to it here serves no meaningful purpose except that an English reader cannot do what he may be most moved to do at the end of the book: to seek out Daumal's other writings. Most readers should turn directly to the text of the novel and come back to these pages afterwards. For in them I have set myself the principal task of tracing the themes of *Mount Analogue* through Daumal's brief life and long work.

I

So I was being observed! I was not alone in that world! That world which I might have taken for sheer personal fantasy. For Nerval has been there and describes just what I have seen and often what happens to me there.

Thus Daumal opens his long essay in tribute to 'Nerval the Nyctalope', the great French romantic poet born exactly 100 years before him. The spiritual link between them is perfectly clear, for both write alternately about and out of 'that world' which lies beyond this one. And neither of them took cover behind the convenient shrubbery of the 'ineffable'; words brought their trials and their triumphs. Daumal's work follows Nerval's in its resolve to fuse body and Spirit, speech and sleep, logic and intuition, in order to enter a 'second life'. Nerval, however, prepared himself increasingly to disappear for good into that other world and finally hung himself in a Paris alley. Daumal, somewhat less afflicted, or blessed, with night vision, resolutely returned to this world, his eyes seeking light again, his mind struggling to tell what he had seen. He was one of the sanest and most wide-awake of men. A letter he addressed at twenty-four to Jean Paulhan makes this declaration: 'I ASSURE YOU THERE WAS FIRE AROUND US IN THE AIR.' Yet two pages later he writes with equal vehemence, 'We must first become human before seeking anything superior.'

Although his spiritual ancestry goes back most directly to Nerval, Daumal's literary forebear by geography is Rimbaud. Born in the northern forests and moors of the Ardennes, they both attended the *lycée* in Charleville and showed astonishing mental powers in early adolescence. At ten Daumal told his parents in a letter, 'I write verses without realizing it.' He continued his education in Reims, but with less and less respect for the conventional frontiers of learning and experience. He later described these years to his physician:

From 15 to 17, at Reims. I began to have doubts, to question the basis of everything. Without giving up my naturally healthy liking for nature, the open air, etc., I began to perform all kinds of experiments 'in order to see.' Along with a few friends (some of the brightest pupils in the *lycée* but all a little wild), I tried alcohol, tobacco, night life, etc. I tried knocking myself out (with Cl^4 or benzene) in order to study just how consciousness disappears and what power I had over it. I became interested in poetry (the *poète maudit* tradition) and philosophy (the 'occultist' tradition) – the way my classmates with religious backgrounds were going in for Satanism. At 17½, for lack of any good reason to go on living, I attempted suicide. Immediately I felt the ties to my family and my responsibility toward my younger brother.

Unsatisfied by his regular studies, Daumal now began learning Sanskrit by himself. Within a few years he had mastered the language and much of its literature, composed a Sanskrit grammar as he went along, and begun a series of translations and revaluations of original texts that he would continue right up to his death. In Paris, where he pushed his studies further into mathematics, science, medicine and philosophy, a bad fall while doing gymnastics deprived him of his memory the first day of competitive examinations for the École Normale Supérieure. He grew to consider this abrupt diversion from a career in 'higher learning' as a fortunate accident. In spite of precarious health and signs of fatigue, he began to experiment with hashish and other drugs in his search for direct experience of truth and at the same time increased his literary activity. Principally, he became one of the most dedicated editors of the review *Le Grand Jeu*.

In 1928 the forces of Dada and surrealism had been making loud noises for ten years and were beginning to be taken seriously by a small public and a growing number of culture speculators. The general staff of surrealism, all men still under forty, had attempted to impose a certain discipline on the avant-garde. Yet in 1928, at a meeting called officially to discuss the attitude surrealism would adopt towards Trotsky's defection and banishment, the obstreperous proceedings were monopolized by the question of whether or not to collaborate with the editors of the new review *Le Grand Jeu*. These young men, acting on the assumption that all the terrain of surrealism had already been conquered and annexed for their generation, had no patience with the eternal wrangling of the surrealists over political affiliation with Communism, personal animosities and purges, and various forms of public posturing. Ten years after its birth, surrealism had no intention of allowing itself to be pushed aside and outdistanced by a few youngsters. It is, of course, exactly what had to happen.

Barely out of their teens, the editors of *Le Grand Jeu* had worked together for four years as a tightly knit group, sharing their intellectual escapades and aspirations, first at the *lycée* in Reims, then as 'free students' in Paris. The original four in Reims, aged sixteen, had called themselves the Simplists: Roger Gilbert-Lecomte, the forceful, erratic leader of the group; Roger Vailland, who went on to win the Prix Goncourt in 1957 with his novel, *The Law*; Robert Meyrat; and René Daumal. Of the four Daumal had the most relentless and best-trained mind.* This *Grand Jeu* group showed such a sure sense of the challenge posed by surrealism and so strong a resolve to stop at nothing in its investigations of human consciousness that it has been described as a 'many-headed Rimbaud'. Far more than the surrealists, they concentrated on group experiments such as meeting in planned dreams and attempting several forms of spiritual and initiatory experience. The dedication and occasional harmfulness of their researches help explain why the two real leaders of the group both died at thirty-six: Gilbert-Lecomte of the effects of morphine addiction, Daumal of tuberculosis.

* A few others joined them: Pierre Minet, A. Rolland de Renéville, J. Sima and Maurice Henry (today a well-known cartoonist).

The labour of bringing out *Le Grand Jeu* and the sustained skirmishes with the surrealists culminated in a lengthy public letter by Daumal to André Breton published in the last number of the review. Daumal takes the movement to task for ineffectuality, ideological poverty and a secret desire for a place in literary history. The fundamental principles of surrealism, its agitation in favour of social and spiritual liberation, he fully approves.

Even though this was an extremely fruitful period in Daumal's literary career, he later wrote of it: 'Violent headaches and anaemia. I wavered between despair and philosophy.' His mind was formed, his future promising – and yet in 1930 he was prepared to throw over everything he had worked to accomplish, just as Rimbaud abandoned literature at a corresponding age. At this juncture, as he relates in several places, Daumal regained his confidence and his sense of direction as a result of meeting a man who appeared to embody the goals that Daumal felt slipping from him. Alexandre de Salzmann was one of the most arresting figures in the community around Gurdjieff. Daumal describes him in a letter as 'a former dervish, former Benedictine, former professor of jujitsu, healer, stage designer, not a tooth left in his head, an incredible man'. The meeting did not so much change Daumal's ideas as reconfirm all the thinking he had done in the previous five years and then begun to doubt. Salzmann directed Daumal's energies with new force towards religion and Oriental philosophy and gave him a sense of the profound importance of the work for which he had been preparing himself since the age of sixteen. Soon after, Daumal married Véra Milanova, a woman deeply in sympathy with his ideas, and settled down at twenty-four to finish his *licence* at the Sorbonne and earn his living in the insecure world of letters.

They were anything but easy years. His military service ended abruptly in a discharge for a heart condition. He produced a series of essays on Nerval, Spinoza, Dalcroze, Hegel, Plato, Sanskrit texts, a wide range of Hindu philosophy and its heresies, and the Western poetic tradition. He worked briefly as press agent for the Indian dancer Uday Shankar and accompanied him to the United States in 1933. For a season the *Nouvelle Revue Française* turned over to Daumal its regular department of short reviews and anecdotes on the contemporary scene, called *'L'Air du Mois'*. His own most regular contribution was 'Pataphysics This Month', a page of comment on the profound absurdity of the latest scientific discoveries and theories. He translated Hemingway's *Death in the Afternoon* and in 1935 received the Jacques Doucet prize awarded by Valéry, Gide and Giraudoux for his first volume of poems, *Le Contre-Ciel* (*Counter-Heaven*). Three years later Gallimard published *La Grande Beuverie* (*A Night of Serious Drinking*), a philosophical and highly imaginative satire of the intellectual environment of Paris. For twenty years it has been a kind of underground text, unforgotten by the generation that lived through the slow disintegration of the thirties. For three years Daumal slaved over the proofs of the first eleven volumes to appear before the war of *L'Encyclopédie Française*. Just before the fall of France an X-ray showed advanced tubercular infection in both lungs. It was during the next four years of perpetual moving, physical debility and uncertain resources that Daumal started, put aside and took up again the writing of *Mount Analogue*. In the intervals he worked as an editor of the literary review *Fontaine*, helped bring out an important number of *Les Cahiers du Sud* on Indian philosophy and religion, and translated three volumes of Suzuki's mammoth opus on Zen Buddhism. He died in occupied Paris on 21 May 1944, two weeks before the Allied landings in Normandy. Eight years later the publisher Gallimard began bringing out all his remaining works, including *Mount Analogue* (1952).

II

By an evolution that testifies to the nature of his character, Daumal's physical appearance grew more commanding, more resolutely masculine and illuminated as his health declined. The reticent, intense young man matured into a challenging bearded figure who impressed his contemporaries as someone who faced the imminence of his death with a deepening concentration of forces in his life. Yet what should hold our attention is not his appearance nor his life nor any single theme in his work. The poems, the philosophical and literary essays, the symbolic tales, the letters, all lead back to a *mind* – unquenchable, fearless, full of human sympathy, devoted to seeking and teaching truth. His least polished and most fragmentary works, of which there are many because of the circumstances of his career, give evidence of the scope of his thought and the range of his knowledge. He was entirely at home in philosophy, science and mathematics. In literature he had absorbed the works of Nerval and Rimbaud and Jarry, three of the most extreme modern visionaries, without losing his perspective on reality and language.

And then there is the Sanskrit, the crushing discipline that prevented his early attraction to Oriental religions from degenerating into a misinformed cultism. Daumal is one of the few men in this century to have combined Eastern and Western thought into something more valuable than a set of personal eccentricities. When he was twenty, he opened a review of a book on the Vedanta by stating: 'The essential weave and texture of my thinking, of our thinking, of all thinking, is written – as I have known for years – in the sacred books of India.' When the Orientalist Jacques Masui met Daumal in Marseilles a few years before his death, he had this impression: 'I can only say that I have never seen a Westerner *live* Indian culture to such a point, so completely that its archetypes must have been there from the beginning.' But what does it mean? What does this Orientalism add up to beyond a collection of esoteric texts? The Westerner tends by tradition to think of grasping the meaning of life through certain crucial experiences: death, grief, danger, passionate love, sudden success, catastrophe. Existentialism has aptly termed them 'extreme situations' in reference to which we discover ourselves – whence our attraction to the adventurous life, war, scientific progress, romantic love. Having cast his mind deep into Indian philosophy, Daumal senses that the reality and meaning of the world can come to us at every moment without our having to rely wholly on extreme situations to wrench us into awareness. Action, as has been pointed out many times, is for Westerners both stimulant and drug. The four stages of Hindu initiation, from the Vedas to the Upanishads, and the complementary disciplines of Yoga and Zen prepare us not for a career of great exploits to be recalled in old age but for a life increasingly dedicated to 'the teaching that cuts through illusion'.

Daumal held these several levels of knowledge in place not only by a keen sensibility and intelligence but also by a sense of ironic perspective on them all – the simple need to laugh finally at the enormous disparity between the particular and the universal, between illusion and truth, between our cross-eyed version of things (by the very fact that we need *two* eyes to see 'straight') and what he facetiously described as the 'objective strabism' inherent in reality. One of his most brilliant demonstrations, called 'The Falsehood of Truth', isolates *error* as the principle of creation and existence, for one tiny truth would obliterate the entire universe by its wonder. This advanced cosmic sense of humour has no other name than Jarry's term, pataphysics. It is probably the most difficult aspect of Daumal's character to combine with the rest, and the most human.

Daumal's waggishness did not prevent him from seeking, seriously, to penetrate the mystery of human thought.* Bio-

* The clearest example in *Mount Analogue can be found in the passage (pp. 69–70)* where Sogol describes the experiments he has performed to measure the power of human thought. The closely connected question of how many related – or in fact unrelated – strands of attention the mind can simultaneously pursue has provided a large area for innovation in the arts: stream of consciousness and automatic writing in literature, multiple perspective in painting, multiple tonality in music, and many more techniques for packing the universe into an instant of intensified consciousness. Daumal was probably right in setting the limit for strictly discursive thought at four; a well-trained conductor, however, can follow as many as six lines of music at once. The question is a significant one for our mental behaviour, and no psychologist can explain to us how we divide and coordinate our attention in such complex actions as looking at the stars, listening to a fugue, or reading an allegory.

graphical facts reveal the outward circumstances of his search. Daumal's first encounter with the reality of life came not in the usual form of awakening desire but as an intense and terrifying awareness of death. And when he had conquered this inner threat by learning to control his physical and nervous system, he went on to overcome the temptation of suicide and later the temptation of drugs. And he had to struggle with the temptation to which poets are prone: the tendency to conceive of life and reality entirely through language. *Mount Analogue*, in its simplicity of expression and universality of meaning, probably represents Daumal's ultimate reckoning with the problem of language, vehicle and obstacle.

Through these stages of inner struggle Daumal became increasingly aware of a mode of mental operation which is not new with him or with the age but which has remained foreign to our activist way of life. He understood very early that the basic act of consciousness is a negation, a dissociation of the *I* from the exterior world of *not-I*. Meaningful perception reduces and refines the *I*, withdraws it from the world into an increasingly strict identity or subjectivity. Then, however, beginning a vibratory rhythm that must follow if self-annihilation is not to result, the pure consciousness expands again into all things, experiences the world subjectively once more, loses itself in the mystery of creation. Baudelaire describes this rhythm of consciousness in the terse words that open *Mon Cœur Mis à Nu: 'De la vaporisation et de la centralisation du* Moi. *Tout est là.'* Daumal would accept the terms and reverse the order. Centralization or concentration: elimination of everything exterior in order to arrive at the intensity of self-awareness. Vaporization: reassimilation of all the universe in the amplitude of sympathy and action. The alternation of contraction and expansion gives human consciousness its rest and motion, its inner time and space, its own East and West. In contrast to Bergson's intuitive surrender to the object of knowledge, Daumal asserts over and over again in poetry and in discourse the essentially masculine, creative, and revelatory act of *negation*, of dissociating the world from ourselves and from itself in a meaningful dialectic, as when God divided light from darkness, the firmament from the waters. This initial stage of consciousness Daumal called an 'asceticism'; only if this ascetic discipline has been achieved can one attempt the opposite and more tempting movement of fusion with all things.

In 1941 the editor of *Les Cahiers de la Pléiade* asked a number of writers to describe the most significant and crucial experience in their life. Most of the others agreed and then begged off; Daumal, spurred by the example of Milosz's *Epistle to Sorge*, produced one of the most authentic and influential texts on extra-rational experience written in this century. In a bare dozen pages Daumal struggles to describe and analyse in rational terms sensations and reflections on the brink of unconsciousness and even death. His youthful experiments with carbon tetrachloride, whose results he has corroborated from other sources, furnish his direct evidence. For nearly twenty years this evidence has left him with the absolute *certainty* (he repeats and underlines the word) of having entered another world. It is not, he insists, the passive, backward-looking world of dreams to which he attained but a realm of superior awareness, which he describes in visual, mathematical and acoustic detail. Is there, then, more than one kind of unconsciousness?

> It is important to repeat that in that new state of being, I perceived and understood perfectly the ordinary state of being, the latter being contained within the former, as waking consciousness contains our unconscious dreams, and not the reverse. This last irreversible relation proves the superiority (in the scale of reality or consciousness) of the first state over the second.*

'A Fundamental Experience' ('*Une Expérience Fondamentale*'), as this essay is called, traces a clear instance of the rhythm of consciousness which I have been describing – first, rigorous consoli-

* A complete translation of the text can be found in *The X Review* (London), 1959. In the last sentence I have corrected an inadvertent error in Daumal's essay reproduced in the published text.

dation of one's identity as an individual, then expansion into a new realm of direct knowledge by semi-intuitive projection (here, artificially induced by toxic action), and then reconsolidation of one's consciousness by rational scrutiny of one's perceptions. This essay is probably the most appropriate of Daumal's works to read after *Mount Analogue*.

From his unflinching investigations of the nature of thought and consciousness Daumal extracted very early the unshakable premises of his philosophy. He rejected any dualistic conception of the universe in favour of a unity of meaning, of existence and of thought. 'Dialectical materialism, carried to its limit, is not essentially different from absolute idealism or from the Vedanta carried to their limits.' Without being a sociologist or a psychologist, Daumal, aged twenty, saw through and attacked Lévy-Bruhl's widely accepted thesis that the primitive mind is different in its operations from the civilized mind – a theory Lévy-Bruhl himself finally had to recant. And the principle on which Daumal and his friends based the entire effort of *Le Grand Jeu* asserted the convergence of the three great approaches to truth: philosophy (especially Plato's dialectic), the 'initiation' of the occult tradition properly understood, and poetry ('a means of achieving sacred knowledge').

This is the heart of Daumal's thinking, the result of experiments performed back and forth across the threshold of his own consciousness, of a wide-ranging knowledge, and of a discipline of mind which usually comes with age and not with youth. Nowhere in his writings does Daumal invoke the doctrines of grace and prayer. He worships no benevolent or anthropomorphic god, nor does he speak of any deity in the Western sense. (His first volume of poems bears the title *Counter-Heaven*, and one of the principal characters in *Mount Analogue* is ironically dubbed Father Sogol.) Man achieves inner spiritual progress by his own efforts, by a human discipline that is not a gift of God and can be learned from other men further advanced on the path of knowledge. Teaching and initiation are central to all religions and cultures. Within a system where no truth comes by divine revelation but only by human attainment, the sense of a tradition of knowledge comes to support the entire structure of life. And thus Daumal spoke unflinchingly of a Doctrine, meaning not a narrow set of rituals or dogmas, not art for art's sake in aesthetics, not a fixed philosophical position, but a number of paths leading to the same goal: a higher form of life.

Personally I can follow Daumal this far (and with some misgivings along the way) only because his discipline as a writer kept him out of the swamps of obscurity and false posturing, and because he never deserted for long the everyday world of shoes and pocket money. Even the insufficiencies of language led him back to it.

> In the process of putting so much pressure on language, thought ceases to be satisfied with the support of words; it bursts away from them in order to seek its resolution elsewhere. This 'elsewhere' should not be understood as a transcendent realm, a mysterious metaphysical domain. This 'elsewhere' is 'here' in the immediacy of real life. It is from *right here* that our thoughts rise up, and it is here that they must come back. But after what travels! Live first; then turn to philosophy; but, in the third place, live again. The man in Plato's cave has to go out and contemplate the light of the sun; then, strengthened by this light, which he keeps in his memory, he has to return to the cave. Verbal philosophy is only a necessary stage in this voyage.

The insistence that the goal of life is not elsewhere but in life itself, in perfecting life, places Daumal closer to Rabelais (for whom he had great admiration) than to Plotinus. *La Grande Beuverie*, for all the rigour of its dissection of contemporary culture, is a rollicking free-for-all full of word play, pastiche and self-irony. It gives in highly entertaining yet serious form the preliminary negative stage of thought. During the course of this imaginary drunk, Daumal examines, caricatures and rejects the diversions and delusions of supposedly intelligent people. And yet this furious humour leads to the conclusion that man, rid of his illusions, can attain to a state of maturity.

III

It should not now seem surprising that at the end of his life Daumal wished to express himself very simply and affirmatively. *Mount Analogue*, the work he then proceeded to write, transposes into fiction his own spiritual autobiography – not only in such passages as the description of his experience of death as a boy and in the resemblance of Sogol to Salzmann but also in the entire movement of the action. (In the summary of events to come, quoted on pages 103–4, he continues to say *we* even when he is writing objectively about the characters in the story.) At the time of the book's appearance in France many reviewers speculated busily over the particular literary genre to which it should be assigned. Most of them settled for the *conte philosophique* in the tradition of Voltaire and Swift, crossed with the marvel tale in the tradition of Cyrano de Bergerac, Poe and Jules Verne. Daumal himself had said he wanted to do for metaphysics what Verne had done for physics. The critics might have mentioned Bunyan and Blake as well. Though extraneous, this discussion served to indicate the richness of Daumal's story: an adventure tale bordering on science fiction, encompassing poetic and broadly comic passages, leading into spiritual quest, and ending . . . ending in the air. The open ending of *Mount Analogue* is only momentarily exasperating; one soon understands that this is the only conclusion that could have kept the book within the domain of literature and at the same time imply a surpassing of any literary form. My only regret is that the break did not occur fifty pages later after Daumal had had time to narrate at least a few days of perilous ascent on the upper slopes. The notes following the novel suggest what he might have written. Ultimately, Daumal's own tongue-in-cheek subtitle turns out to be an accurate designation after all: 'A Novel of Symbolically Authentic Non-Euclidean Adventures in Mountain Climbing.'

Mount Analogue is a marvel tale, yet every strand of the story arises out of a perfectly credible psychological situation. At the opening of the story the narrator has published, and forgotten, an article he wrote in half-amused speculation and in which he 'never really believed'. Yet by the irony of human error, that article opens the door to final truth. By a similar irony the only external threat to the expedition comes from some of the original members who betray its goals and form a rival expedition. Even though a spiritual adventure is being related, Daumal comes back several times to the practical and symbolic consideration of money. The unique financial structure of the island of Mount Analogue, far from supporting a material commerce only, derives from and leads back to the highest aspirations of the community. A few unpretentious words on pages 43–4 repeat the refrain of Daumal's thought: growing up in modern Western civilization obliges us to extinguish certain faculties and to retreat within a pattern of experience that cuts us off from most spiritual knowledge. *Mount Analogue* speaks of voyage and liberation in a soft voice that draws one closer to hear.

The most deadly sin, the insidious pride that comes closest to causing the downfall of the expedition, appears in the form of *libido sciendi*, the lust to know. The theme works particularly well, for in the early stages of the story such scientific questions as the curvature of space, high-altitude survival and linguistic shift on the island play a role both in the outward circumstances of the action and in its symbolic ramifications. As time goes on, however, knowledge in the scientific sense becomes meaningless, and each individual finds himself confronted by the single responsibility to advance, in concert with a few companions, towards a snowy peak in a black sky. Early in the story we are given a picture of the most inhuman of environments: a monastic order corrupted by mutual distrust and denunciation. Later, on the slopes of Mount Analogue, a sense of community emerges as one of the highest forms of knowledge.

The central metaphor of the mountain scarcely needs the justification Daumal gives it in the opening pages. His gifts as a poet allow him to put to vivid use the details of landscape and atmosphere, the dangers and hardships of mountain climbing. The adventures recounted here, symbolic as they may be, never cease to be concerned with frozen toes and heavy packs as well as with the stages of a spiritual quest. There is some mention of a 'higher will' having sway over the island, but a will that confines its acts to preparing the circumstances under which each man will seek his salvation. Thus, the most moving scene in Daumal's novel occurs when Sogol, in a moment of triumph and humility and insight, finds the first 'peradam', a precious stone peculiar to Mount Analogue. In that moment he is reborn and discovers his identity. The later chapters, if written, would probably have described a corresponding transformation in each of the other characters.

I cannot help seeing *Mount Analogue* as itself a peradam in the stony fields of literature. The peradam possesses such perfect transparence that it escapes the notice of all except those who are inwardly prepared and outwardly situated to catch sight of its glint. Its discovery and possession give evidence of true election among men and confer inner peace. And the peradam, as we are told in the heading of the uncompleted Chapter 5, can curve and uncurve space because of its unique index of refraction. *Mount Analogue,* the novel, has the force of a curving and uncurving lens for our minds. Through it we can glimpse that 'other world' of which Nerval spoke, and Spinoza and Socrates. And yet it is hard to look through it, for so limpid a substance almost escapes one's attention even when it is right under one's eyes. One could conceivably read every word of the book without 'seeing' a thing.

Because of the book's truncated form, one aspect of its 'curvature' comes into full sight only in Daumal's summary of the remaining action. 'Before setting out for the next refuge, one must prepare those coming after to occupy the place one is leaving.' When we reach this passage, we have just been prepared; for *Mount Analogue* itself embodies the 'knowledge to be passed on to other seekers'. We have been shown what it is only too human to forget: that between learning and teaching there exists no secure and stationary zone of knowledge. To know means to be learning or to be teaching; there is no middle way. The human mind enjoys no state of passive grace. Yet, beyond a certain point, teaching becomes a very subtle and deceptive undertaking, scarcely to be distinguished from learning. 'Socrates,' Daumal writes, 'never teaches anything. He plays the fool and from time to time tells a legend, assuring us that it's just for his own amusement.' So Daumal, too, with obvious relish, tells us a legend in which we find not doctrine but a sturdy weave of action and reflection, not thoughts only but men thinking.

ROGER SHATTUCK
Aix-en-Provence, 1959

Works by Daumal

Le Contre-Ciel, Cahiers Jacques Doucet, 1936. Reissued 1970 with *Les dernières paroles du poète.*

La Grande Beuverie, Gallimard, 1938. Reissued in 1977 edited by Claudio Rugafiori.

Le Mont Analogue: Récit Véridique, Preface by A. Rolland de Renéville. Postface by Véra Daumal. Gallimard, 1952.

Chaque Fois Que l'Aube Paraît: Essais et Notes, Vol. I. Gallimard, 1953.

Lettres à Ses Amis, Vol. I. Gallimard, 1958.

Poésie Noire, Poésie Blanche, Gallimard, 1959.

Bharata: L'Origine du Théâtre; La Poésie et la Musique en Inde; Traductions de Textes Sacrés et Profanes, Introduction by Jacques Masui. Gallimard, 1970.

Tu T'es Toujours Trompé, Edited by Jack Daumal. Mercure de France, 1970.

L'Évidence Absurde: Essais et Notes, Vol. I (1926–1934). Edited by Claudio Rugafiori. Gallimard, 1972.

Les Pouvoirs de la Parole: Essais et Notes, Vol. II (1935–1943). Edited by Claudio Rugafiori. Gallimard, 1972; reissued 1982.

With Roger Gilbert-Lecomte, *Le Grand Jeu*, facsimile edition, J. Place, 1977.

René Daumal ou le retour à soi with *Textes et études sur son oeuvre*, Original, 1981.

Mugle, Fata Morgana, 1978.

Works on Daumal

Biès, Jean. *René Daumal.* Collection 'Poètes d'Aujourd'hui.' Pierre Seghers, 1967. Bibliography. Reissued 1973.

'La Voie de René Daumal.' Special number of *Hermès*, No. 5, 1967.

'René Daumal.' Special number of *La Grive*, Nos. 135–6, 1967.

'Le Grand Jeu.' Special number of *L'Herne*, No. 10, 1968.

Jean Neaumet, *René Daumal et les authorismes*, thesis, Université de Paris, 1976.

Gérard Duithard, *René Daumal: Langage et Connaissance – Recherche d'une poetique*, thesis, Université de Tours, 1980.

Translation

A Night of Serious Drinking (La Grande Beuverie), translated by David Coward and E. A. Lovatt, Routledge & Kegan Paul Ltd, 1979.

MOUNT ANALOGUE

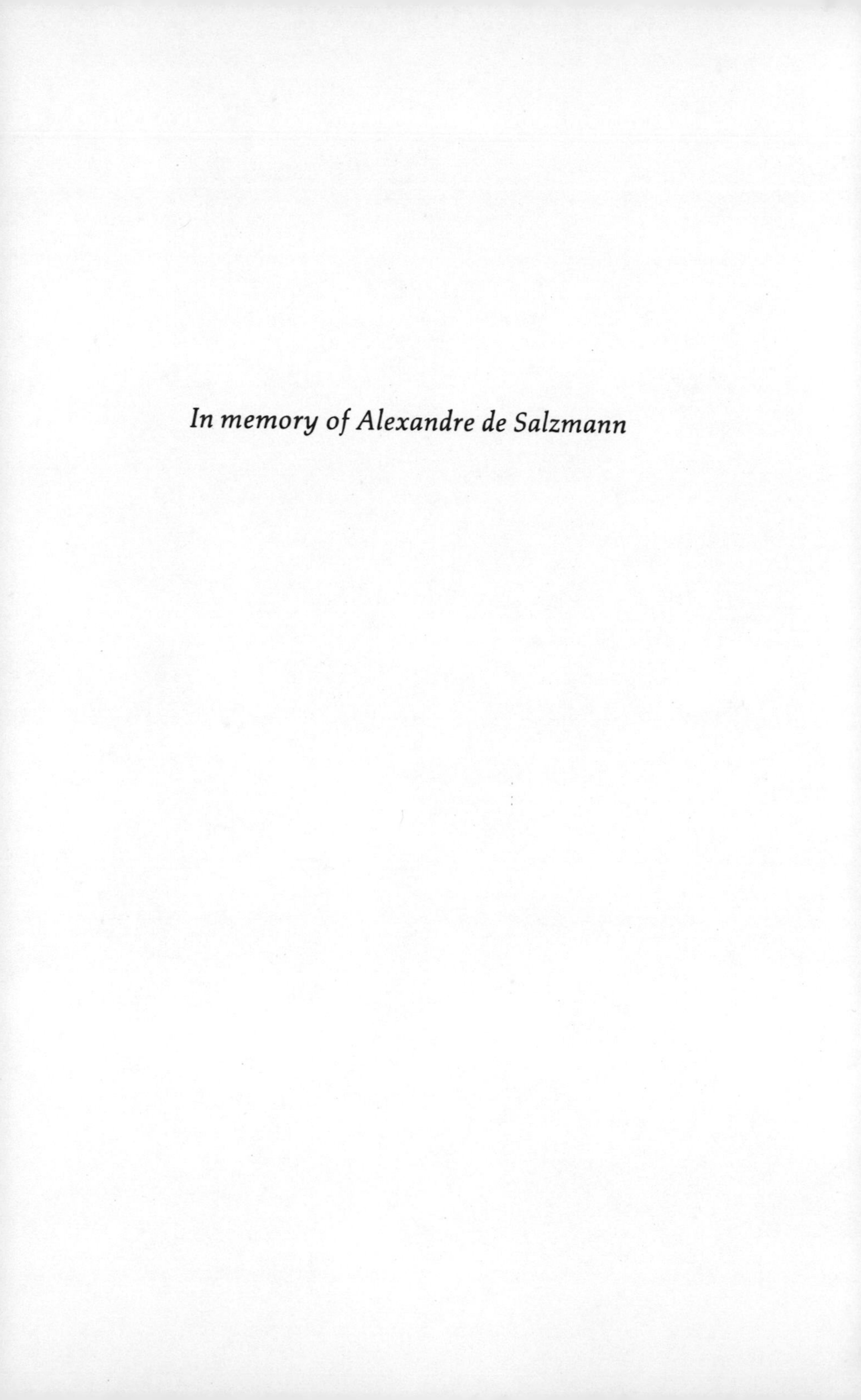

In memory of Alexandre de Salzmann

1
Which Is the Chapter of the Meeting

A new development in the author's life – Symbolic mountains – A serious reader – Mountain climbing in the Passage des Patriarches – Father Sogol – An interior park and an exterior brain – The art of getting acquainted – The man who turns ideas inside out – Confidences – A satanic monastery – How the devil on duty led an ingenious monk into temptation – Physics, the industrious – Father Sogol's affliction – A story about flies – The fear of death – With a furious heart, a mind of steel – A crazy plan, reduced to a simple problem of triangulation – A psychological law

My story begins with some unfamiliar handwriting on an envelope. On it was written only my name and the address of the *Revue des Fossiles,* to which I had contributed and from which the letter had been forwarded. Yet those few pen strokes conveyed a shifting blend of violence and gentleness. Beneath my curiosity about the possible sender and contents of the letter, a vague but powerful presentiment evoked in me the image of 'a pebble in the millpond'. And from deep within me, like a bubble, rose the admission that my life had become all too stagnant lately. Thus, when I opened the letter, I could not be sure whether it affected me like a breath of fresh air or like a disagreeable draught.

In what seemed a single movement, the same fluent hand had written as follows:

Sir:

I have read your article on Mount Analogue. Until now I had believed myself the only person convinced of its existence. Today there are two of us, tomorrow there will be ten, perhaps more, and we can attempt the expedition. We must meet without delay. Telephone me as soon as you can at one of the numbers below. I shall be expecting your call.

Pierre Sogol
37 Passage des Patriarches
Paris

[Then followed five or six telephone numbers that I could call at different times of day.]

I had almost forgotten the article to which my correspondent alluded and which had appeared about three months earlier in the May number of the *Revue des Fossiles.*

Though flattered by this evidence of interest on the part of an unknown reader, it made me more than a little uneasy that someone should have taken seriously, almost tragically, a literary fantasy by which I had been carried away at the time, but which had already faded in my memory.

I re-read the article. It was a rather hasty study of the symbolic significance of the mountain in ancient mythologies. The different branches of symbol interpretation had for a long time been my favourite field of study; I naively believed I understood something about the subject. Furthermore, I had an alpinist's passionate love of mountains. The convergence of these two contrasting areas of interest on the same object, the mountain, had given certain passages of my article a lyric tone. (Such conjunctions, incongruous as they may appear, play a large part in the genesis of what is commonly called poetry; I venture this remark as a suggestion to critics and aestheticians who seek to illuminate the depths of that mysterious language.)

I had written in substance that in the mythic tradition the Mountain is the bond between Earth and Sky. Its solitary summit reaches the sphere of eternity, and its base spreads out in manifold foothills into the world of mortals. It is the way by which man can raise himself to the divine and by which the divine can reveal itself to man. The patriarchs and prophets of the Old Testament behold the Lord face to face in high places. For Moses it was Mount Sinai and Mount Nebo; in the New Testament it is the Mount of Olives and Golgotha. I went so far as to discover this ancient symbol of the mountain in the pyramidal constructions of Egypt and Chaldea. Turning to the Aryans, I recalled those obscure legends of the Vedas in which the soma – the 'nectar' that is the 'seed of immortality' – is said to reside in its luminous and subtle form 'within the mountain'. In India the Himalayas are the dwelling place of Siva, of his spouse 'the Daughter of the Mountain', and of the 'Mothers' of all worlds, just as in Greece the king of the gods held court on Mount Olympus. In fact it was in Greek mythology that I found the symbol completed by the story of the revolt of the children of Earth who, with their terrestrial natures and terrestrial means, attempted to scale Olympus and enter Heaven on feet of clay. Was not this the same endeavour as that of the builders of the Tower of Babel, who, without renouncing their many personal ambitions, aspired to attain the kingdom of the one impersonal Being? In China people have always referred to the 'Mountains of the Blessed', and the ancient sages instructed their disciples on the edge of a precipice.

After having surveyed the best-known mythologies, I went on to a general discussion of symbols, which I divided into two classes: those subject only to the law of 'proportion' and those subject to the law of 'scale' as well. This distinction has often been made. Nevertheless I shall restate it: 'Proportion' concerns the relations between dimensions of a structure, 'scale' the relations between these dimensions and those of the human body. An equilateral triangle, symbol of the Trinity, has exactly the same value no matter what its dimensions; it has no 'scale'. On the other hand, consider an exact model of a cathedral a few inches in height. This object will always convey, through its shape and proportions, the intellectual meaning of the original structure, even if some details have to be examined under a magnifying glass. But it will no longer produce anything like the same emotion or the same response: It is no longer 'to scale'. And what defines the scale of the ultimate symbolic mountain – the one I propose to call Mount Analogue – is its *inaccessibility to ordinary human approaches*. Now, Sinai, Nebo and Olympus have long since become what mountaineers call cow pastures; and even the highest peaks of the Himalayas are no longer considered inaccessible today. All these summits have therefore lost their analogical importance. The symbol has had to take refuge in totally mythical mountains, such as Mount Meru of the Hindus. But, to take this one example, if Meru has no geographical location, it loses its persuasive significance as a *way uniting Earth and Heaven*; it can still represent the centre or axis of our planetary system but no longer the means whereby man can attain it.

'For a mountain to play the role of Mount Analogue,' I concluded, *'its summit must be inaccessible, but its base accessible* to human beings as nature has made them. It must be *unique*, and it must *exist geographically*. The door to the invisible must be visible.'

That is what I had written. Taken literally, my article did indeed imply that I believed in the existence, somewhere on the surface of the globe, of a mountain far higher than Mount Everest – a belief that was, to any so-called sensible person, absurd. And here was someone taking me at my word and talking about 'attempting an expedition'! A lunatic? A practical joker? But what about myself, I thought suddenly; didn't my readers have the right to ask the same questions of me, who had written the article? All right, am I a lunatic or a practical joker? Or just a man of letters? Well, I can admit to it now, while asking myself these disagreeable questions, I felt that in spite of everything *some part of me deep down firmly believed in the material existence of Mount Analogue*.

The following morning I called the telephone number indicated for that hour in the letter. An impersonal woman's voice suddenly blurted out 'Eurhyne Laboratories' and asked with whom I wished to speak. After a little clicking a man's voice came through.

'Ah! So it's you? It's a lucky thing for you the telephone doesn't transmit smells. Will you be free Sunday? . . . Come to my place around eleven, then. We'll take a little stroll in my park before lunch . . . What? Yes, of course, Passage des Patriarches, why? . . . Oh! The park? That's my laboratory. I thought you were a mountaineer . . . Yes? Well, then, it's all agreed . . . See you Sunday.'

So, he's not a lunatic. A lunatic wouldn't have an important position in a perfume factory. A practical joker? That warm, forceful voice did not belong to a prankster. That was Thursday. Three days of waiting, during which people found me very distracted.

Sunday morning, kicking tomatoes, slipping on banana peels, jostling sweaty housewives, I made my way to the Passage des Patriarches. Entering the building through an archway, I communed with the soul of empty corridors and was finally drawn to a door at the far end of the court. Before opening it, I noticed two strands of rope which hung down across the face of the bulging decrepit wall from a little window on the sixth floor. A pair of corduroy breeches – as far as I could tell at that distance – emerged out of the window. These tucked into long stockings that disappeared into soft shoes. The person so attired at the lower extremity, while hanging on to the sill of the window with one hand, wound the two lines of the rope through his legs, then around his right thigh, then obliquely across his chest to the left shoulder, then over the turned-up collar of his short jacket, and finally down in front across his right shoulder – all this with a flick of his wrist. He grasped the lines below him with his right hand and those above with his left hand, pushed himself away from the wall with his feet, and with erect torso and spread legs, descended at a speed of five feet a second, in the style that looks so well in photographs. He had scarcely touched the ground when a second figure started out over the same course. But on arriving at the bulge in the old wall, this second person was struck on the head with something resembling a rotten potato, which squashed itself on the pavement below while a voice from up above trumpeted, 'To get you used to falling rock!' All the same, he reached the bottom without being too disconcerted but did not finish his *rappel de corde* with the movement which justifies that name and which consists in pulling on one of the lines to retrieve the rope. The two men sauntered off under the disgusted gaze of the concierge. Going through the door, I climbed four flights of service stairs and came upon these words on a sign posted next to the window:

Pierre Sogol, Professor of Mountaineering. Lessons Thursday and Sunday, from 7 to 11 A.M. Means of access: Go out of the window, take a left turn, scale a chimney on to the cornice, climb a crumbling schist slope, follow the ridge from north to south, avoiding several gendarmes, and enter by the skylight on the east slope.

I willingly submitted to these fantasies, even though the stairs went on up to the sixth floor. The 'turn' was a narrow ledge along the wall, the 'chimney' a dark recess that needed only to be closed by the construction of an adjoining building to be called a court, the 'schist slope' a dilapidated slate roof, and the 'faults' some mitred and peaked chimneys. I entered through the skylight and found myself face to face with the man himself. Fairly tall, lean, and vigorous, with a heavy black moustache and wavy hair, he had the tranquillity of a caged panther biding his time. He looked at me with calm dark eyes and held out his hand.

'You see what I have to do to make a living,' he said. 'I'd like to receive you in better quarters –'

'I thought you worked in a perfume laboratory,' I interrupted.

'That's only part of the story. I do odd jobs in a domestic appliance factory, a camping-goods store, a laboratory producing insecticide, and a photo-engraving company. In each one I undertake reputedly impossible inventions. Up to now I've managed, but since they know I can't do any other kind of work in life except invent absurdities, they pay me badly. So I give climbing lessons to sons of the idle rich, bored with bridge and travelling. Make yourself at home and have a look around my garret.'

The place consisted of several attic rooms with the partitions knocked out to make a long low studio, lit and ventilated by a huge window at one end. Under the window were piled up the usual apparatus of a physiochemical laboratory. Through the studio wound a pebble path, devious as the track of an onery mule and bordered with shrubs and bushes in pots or in crates, cactus plants, small conifers, dwarf palms, and rhododendrons. Along the path, glued to the window panes or hung on the bushes or dangling from the ceiling, so that all free space was put to maximum use, hundreds of little placards were displayed. Each one carried a drawing, a photograph, or an inscription, and the whole constituted a veritable encyclopaedia of what we call human knowledge. A diagram of a plant cell, Mendeleev's periodic table of the elements, the keys to Chinese writing, a cross-section of the human heart, Lorentz's transformation formulae, each planet and its characteristics, fossil remains of the horse species in series, Mayan hieroglyphics, economic and demographic statistics, musical phrases, samples of the principal plant and animal families, crystal specimens, the ground plan of the Great Pyramid, brain diagrams, logistic equations, phonetic charts of the sounds employed in all languages, maps, genealogies – everything in short which would fill the brain of a twentieth-century Pico della Mirandola.

Here and there, jars, aquariums and cages held various extravagant fauna. But my host did not let me linger over his holothurians, his calamary, his water-spiders, his termites, his ant-lions and his axolotls; he led me on to the path where the two of us could just stand abreast and asked me to take a stroll with him around the laboratory. Thanks to a slight cross draught and the scent of the dwarf conifers, one had the impression of climbing the zigzags of an interminable mountain path.

'You understand,' Pierre Sogol said to me, 'that you and I have such grave decisions to make, with such far-reaching consequences for our lives, that we can't start by taking shots in the dark. We'll have to get to know each other. Today we can walk around together, talk, eat, and be silent together. Later I believe we'll have the opportunity to act and suffer together. All that is necessary to "make someone's acquaintance", as they say.'

Naturally we talked of mountains. He had explored all the highest ranges on our planet, and I had the feeling that with one of us at each end of a stout rope, we could that very day have attempted the most dangerous ascents. Then the conversation jumped, veered off in several directions, and reversed itself, and I began to understand the use to which he put all those pieces of cardboard which spread out before us the knowledge of the century. All of us keep a fairly extensive collection of such diagrams and inscriptions in our heads; and we have the illusion we are 'thinking' the loftiest scientific and philosophical thoughts when, by chance, a few of them fall into a pattern that seems neither too conventional nor too novel. It happens as if by the effect of draughts or cross-currents or simply by the result of their own constant shiftings, like the Brownian movement, which displaces particles suspended in a liquid. Here, all this material was visibly outside of us; we could not confuse it with ourselves. As a garland is strung from hooks, we hung our conversation on these little images, and each of us could see the mechanism of the other's mind and of his own with equal clarity.

As in all his outward appearance, there was in this man's manner of thinking a singular combination of vigorous maturity and the freshness of a child. But above all, just as I was aware of the action of his restless and untiring legs, I was aware also of his thinking, like a force as palpable as heat or light or wind. This force seemed to consist in an exceptional faculty for seeing ideas as external objects and for establishing new links between ideas that appeared totally unrelated. I heard him – I'd be prepared to say I saw him – treat human history as a problem in descriptive geometry, then a moment later speak of the properties of numbers in terms of zoological species. The fusion and division of cells became a particular instance of logical reasoning, and language obeyed the same laws as celestial mechanics.

I had difficulty answering him and soon found myself becoming slightly giddy. He noticed and began to speak of his past life.

'While still quite young,' he said, 'I had already experienced almost every pleasure and every disappointment, every happiness and every suffering, which can befall a man as a social animal. It would be useless to give you the details: the repertory of possible happenings in a human life is fairly limited, and it always comes down to about the same story. It's enough to say that one day I found myself alone and fully convinced that I had finished one cycle of existence. I had travelled a great deal, studied a variety of improbable sciences, learned ten odd trades. Life dealt with me a little the way an organism treats a foreign body: it was obviously trying either to encyst me or to expel me, and for my own part I yearned for "something else". After a time I believed I had found that "something else" in religion. I entered a monastery, a very strange one. Its name and location make little difference; but, to say the least, it belonged to a distinctly heretical order.

'In particular there was a curious custom in the rule of the order. Every morning our Superior handed to each of us – we were about thirty in all – a slip of paper folded twice. One of these slips bore the words "*Tu hodie*", and only the Superior knew which of us received it. Moreover I believe that on certain days all the slips were blank, but since no one knew, the result was the same, as you'll see. "Your turn today" – it meant that the brother so designated, without the others' knowing it, would play the part of "Tempter" all that day. In certain African tribes and elsewhere I've witnessed some fairly horrible rituals, such as human sacrifices and cannibalistic rites. But in no religious sect or practice of witchcraft have I ever encountered so cruel a custom as this institution of the daily Tempter. Can you imagine thirty men leading a communal life, already half-crazed by the perpetual terror of sinning, looking at one another obsessed by the knowledge that one of them, they don't know who, has been specially commissioned to test their faith, their humility, and their charity? It was like a diabolic caricature of a compelling idea – the idea that in my fellow man as in myself there is both a person to hate and a person to love.

'For one thing proves to me the diabolical nature of this custom: not one of all the brothers ever refused to accept the role of Tempter. No one, when the *Tu hodie* was given to him, had the slightest doubt that he was capable and worthy of playing the part. The Tempter was himself the victim of a monstrous temptation. Several times, out of obedience to the order, I too accepted the role of agent provocateur; it's the most shameful memory of my life. I accepted until one day I realized the trap I had fallen into. Up to that point I had always spotted these second-hand Satans. They were so naive and always tried the same tricks, which they believed to be very subtle, poor devils. Their entire approach consisted of variations on a few fundamental falsehoods everyone knew, such as "To obey the letter of the rules is only for imbeciles who cannot understand their spirit" or "With my health, alas, I cannot attempt such hardships."

'One time, though, the devil on duty succeeded in catching me. That day it was a big jolly rough-hewn fellow with baby-blue eyes. During a rest period he strolled up to me. "I see you've spotted me," he said. "There's no way of getting by you; you notice too much. Anyway, you don't need this kindergarten game to tell you that temptation is forever around us, or rather within us. But just think of the unfathomable laziness of man; all the schemes which are supposed to keep him awake and watchful end up by putting him to sleep. We wear a hairshirt the way we might wear a monocle; we sing matins the way other people play golf. If only scientists today, instead of constantly inventing new means to make life easier, would devote their resourcefulness to producing instruments for rousing man out of his torpor! There are machine guns, of course, but that's going a bit too far . . ."

'He spoke so convincingly that that same evening I obtained from the Superior permission to devote my leisure to inventing and constructing such instruments. My brain was in a fever. I immediately invented some appalling devices: a pen for facile writers which spattered or blotted every five or ten minutes; a tiny portable phonograph, equipped with an earpiece like those on hearing aids and which would cry out at the most unexpected moments: "Who do you think you are?"; a pneumatic cushion that I called "the soft pillow of doubt" and which deflated unexpectedly under the sleeper's head; a mirror whose curvature was designed – and what trouble it gave me – so as to reflect any human face like a pig's head. There were many more. I kept so hard at work I had no time any more to spot the daily tempters. They had a good time egging me on. Then one morning I received the *Tu hodie*. The first brother I met was the big fellow with the baby-blue eyes. He greeted me with a suspicious smile which brought me to my senses. All at once I understood both the childishness of my inventions and the ignominy of the role I was expected to play. Breaking all the rules, I went to find the Superior and told him that I could no longer consent to play the Devil. He spoke to me with mild severity, perhaps sincere, perhaps professional. "My son," he concluded, "I see that there is in you an *incurable need to understand*, which must prevent you from remaining any longer in this house. We shall pray God to call you to Him by other paths."

'That night I took the train for Paris. I had entered the monastery under the name of Brother Petrus. I came out with the title of Father Sogol, and I have kept that pseudonym. The other monks called me that because of a turn of mind they noticed in me which led me to reverse, on a trial basis at least, any statement proposed to me, to invert cause and effect, principle and consequence, substance and accident. "Sogol" is a rather childish anagram and somewhat pretentious, but I needed a name with a good ring to it, and it reminded me of a rule of thought which had served me well. Thanks to my scientific and technical knowledge, I soon found jobs in various laboratories and industrial plants. I readjusted little by little to contemporary life, but only externally, it's true. For when you come down to it, I can't bring myself to fall in with this monkey-cage agitation which people so dramatically call life.'

A bell rang.

'All right, Physics my girl,' Father Sogol called. And he explained to me, 'Dinner's ready. Let's go in.'

He led me off the path and with a gesture indicating all contemporary human knowledge written on the little rectangles before our eyes, said in a grave voice: 'Fake, all fake. I can't say of one of those cards: here's a truth, one small but certain truth. In the whole show there's nothing but mystery and error. Where one ends, the other begins.'

We went into a small room, all white, where the table was set.

'Now here, at least,' he said, 'is something *relatively real*, if one can risk combining these two words without causing an explosion.' We sat down facing one another across one of those fine country stews in which every vegetable in season weaves its savour around a piece of boiled animal. 'My good Physics still has to use all her old Breton skill to put on this table a meal in which there is no barium sulphate, no gelatin, no boric acid, no sulphuric acid, no formaldehyde, and none of the other drugs now used by the food industry. A good stew is worth more than a false philosophy.'

We ate in silence. My host felt no obligation to talk during the meal, and I thought well of him for that. He was not afraid to keep silent when there was nothing to say nor to reflect before speaking. In reporting our conversation now, I fear I have given the impression that he just ran on; in reality his stories and confidences were broken by long silences, and I had spoken fairly often myself. I had given him the general outline of my life, which is not worth reproducing here. As to the silences, how can one describe them with words? Only poetry could do that.

After the meal we returned to the 'park' under the window and stretched out on some rugs and leather cushions: It is a simple way of making a low-ceilinged room seem more spacious. Physics silently brought the coffee, and Sogol began to talk again.

'That fills my stomach, but scarcely more. With a little money in this galloping civilization of ours, one can easily obtain the basic physical satisfactions. The rest is fraud. Fraud, ticks and tricks – there's our whole life, from diaphragm to cranium. My Superior was right: I suffer from an incurable need to understand. I don't want to die without having understood why I lived. What about you? Have you ever been afraid of death?'

In silence I hunted around among my memories, deep memories where words had never before pried. And I spoke with difficulty. 'Yes. When I was around six, I heard something about flies which sting you when you're asleep. And naturally someone dragged in the old joke: "When you wake up, you're dead." The words haunted me. That evening in bed, with the light out, I tried to picture death, the "no more of anything". In my imagination I did away with all the outward circumstances of my life and felt myself confined in ever-tightening circles of anguish: there was no longer any "I" . . . What does it mean, "I"? I couldn't succeed in grasping it. "I" slipped out of my thoughts like a fish out of the hands of a blind man, and I couldn't sleep. For three years these nights of questioning in the dark recurred fairly frequently. Then, one particular night, a marvellous idea came to me: instead of just enduring this agony, try to observe it, to see where it comes from and what it is. I perceived that it all seemed to come from a tightening of something in my stomach, as well as under my ribs and in my throat. I remembered that I was subject to angina and forced myself to relax, especially my abdomen. The anguish disappeared. When I tried again in this new condition to think about death, instead of being clawed by anxiety, I was filled with an entirely new feeling. I knew no name for it – a feeling between mystery and hope.'

'And then you grew up, went to school, and began to "philosophize", didn't you? We all go through the same thing. It seems that during adolescence a person's inner life is suddenly weakened, stripped of its natural courage. In his thinking he no longer dares stand face to face with reality or mystery; he begins to see them through the opinions of "grown-ups", through books and courses and professors. Still, a voice remains which is not completely muffled and which cries out every so often – every time its gag is loosened by an unexpected jolt in the routine. The voice cries out its great questioning of everything, but we stifle it again right away. Well, we already understand each other a little. I can admit to you that I fear death. Not what we *imagine* about death, for such fear is itself imaginary. And not my death as it will be set down with a date in the public records. But that death I suffer every moment, the death of that voice which, out of the depths of my childhood, keeps questioning me as it does you: "Who am I?" Everything in and around us seems to conspire to strangle it once and for all. Whenever that voice is silent – and it doesn't speak often – I'm an empty body, a perambulating carcass. I'm afraid that one day it will fall silent forever, or that it will speak too late – as in your story about the flies: When you wake up, you're dead.

'Well, there it is!' he said, almost violently. 'I've told you the essential thing. Everything else is mere detail. I've been waiting years to say all this to someone.'

He had sat down, and I saw that this man must have a mind of steel to be able to hold on to his sanity. Now he seemed a little relaxed, almost relieved.

'My only good moments,' he continued, after having shifted position, 'used to come in the summer, when I got out my hobnailed boots, knapsack, and ice-axe to have a go at the mountains. I never had long vacations, but I made the most of them. After ten or eleven months spent perfecting vacuum cleaners or synthetic perfumes, after a night in the train and a day in the bus, then arriving with my muscles still all foul with the poisons of the city – well, the first snow fields were often enough to make me cry like a fool, feeling my head empty, my limbs groggy, and my heart wide open to everything. A few days later, wedged into a crevice or astride a ridge, I would come to myself again, I would recognize in myself the persons I had not seen since the previous summer. But in the end it was always the same people . . .

'Now, like you, in my reading and in my travels I had heard about a superior type of man, possessing the keys to everything which is a mystery to us. This idea of a higher and unknown strain within the human race was not something I could take simply as an allegory. Experience had proved, I told myself, that a man cannot reach truth directly nor all by himself. An intermediary has to be present, a force still human in certain respects yet transcending humanity in others. Somewhere on our Earth this superior form of humanity must exist, and not utterly out of our reach. In that case shouldn't all my efforts be directed towards discovering it? Even if, in spite of my certainty, I were the victim of a monstrous illusion, I should lose nothing in the attempt. For apart from this hope, all life lacked meaning for me.

'But where was I to look? Where could I begin? I had already covered the world, poked my nose into everything, into all kinds of religious sects and mystic cults. But with all of them it came down to the same dilemma: maybe yes, maybe no. Why should I stake my life on this one rather than on that one? You see, I had no touchstone. But the very fact that there are now *two of us* changes everything. The task doesn't become twice as easy: After having been *impossible*, it has become *possible*. It's as if you first gave me, in order to measure the distance from a star to our planet, *one* known point on the surface of the globe. You can't make the calculation. Give me a second point, and it becomes possible, for then I can construct the triangle.'

This abrupt switch into geometry was just like him. I don't know if I understood him very well, and I learned later that there was a tiny error in his reasoning. But it had a forcefulness that convinced me.

'Your article on Mount Analogue enlightened me,' he continued. 'The place exists. Both of us *know* that. Therefore we'll discover it. Where? That's a matter of calculation. In a few days, I promise you, I'll have determined its geographic position within a few degrees. And you're ready to start out right away, aren't you?'

'Yes, but how? By what route, by what means of transportation, with what money, for how long?'

'Those are all details. Furthermore, I'm sure we'll not be alone. Two people convince a third, and it all snowballs – even though we'll have to reckon with what people call common sense. It's common sense for water to flow, but just put it on the fire to boil or in a refrigerator to freeze . . . So if there's no fire, we'll have to strike the iron till it heats up. Let's have the first meeting here next Sunday. I have five or six good friends whom I can count on. One is in England and two in Switzerland, but they'll be here. It's always been agreed among us that we'd never attempt a major expedition without the others. And this will be a major expedition if there ever was one.'

'I have a few people in mind, too,' I said.

'Invite them for four o'clock, but come earlier yourself, around two. My calculations will be finished. Well, do you have to leave so soon? All right, here's the exit,' he said, showing me the little window out of which hung the *corde de rappel*. 'Only Physics uses the stairs. Good-bye!'

Using the rope, which smelled of grass and stables, I reached the ground in a few moments.

With a feeling of not belonging, I found myself out in the street, slipping on banana peels, kicking tomatoes, and jostling sweaty housewives.

If, on the way back from the Passage des Patriarches to my apartment near Saint-Germain-des-Prés, I had thought of examining myself like a transparent foreign body, I should have discovered one of the laws which governs the behaviour of 'featherless bipeds unequipped to conceive the number π' – Father Sogol's definition of the species to which he, you and I belong. This law might be termed: inner resonance to influences nearest at hand. The guides on Mount Analogue, who explained it to me later, called it simply the *chameleon law*. Father Sogol had really convinced me, and while he was talking to me, I was prepared to follow him in his crazy expedition. But as I neared home, where I would again find all my old habits, I imagined my colleagues at the office, the writers I knew, and my best friends listening to an account of the conversation I had just had. I could imagine their sarcasm, their scepticism, and their pity. I began to suspect myself of naiveté and credulity, so much so that when I tried to tell my wife about meeting Father Sogol, I caught myself using expressions like 'a funny old fellow', 'an unfrocked monk', 'a slightly daffy inventor', 'a crazy idea'. After all that I was stupefied to hear her say at the end of my story: 'Well, he's right. I'm going to start packing my trunk tonight. For there are not just two of you. There are already three of us!'

'So you take it all seriously?'

'This is the first serious idea I've come across in my life.'

And the force of the chameleon law is so great that I came back to the thought that Father Sogol's enterprise was, after all, entirely reasonable.

*That is how the plan for an expedition to Mount Analogue was born. Now that I have started, I shall have to tell the rest: how it was proved that a hitherto unknown continent really existed, with mountains much higher than the Himalayas; how it happened that no one had detected it before; how we reached it; what creatures we met there; how another expedition, pursuing quite different goals, barely missed destruction; how we have begun little by little to put down roots, so to speak, in this new world; and how, nevertheless, the journey has barely begun . . .

On high, remote in the sky, above and beyond successive circles of increasingly lofty peaks buried under whiter and whiter snows, in a splendour the eye cannot look on, invisible through excess of light, rises the uttermost pinnacle of Mount Analogue.

* The following passages were originally published as the conclusion of Chapter 1 as it appeared in the French periodical *Mesures* (Winter, 1940). [Translator's note.]

There, on a summit more pointed than the finest needle,
He who fills all space resides unto himself.
On high in the most rarefied air, where all freezes into stone,
The supreme and immutable crystal alone subsists.
Up there, exposed to the full fire of the firmament, where all is consumed in flame,
Subsists the perpetual incandescence.
There, at the centre of all creation, is he
Who sees each thing accomplished in its beginning and its end.

That is what the mountain people chant up there. That's what it's like.

You say, that's what it's like;
But if it gets a little cold, your heart turns into a mole;
If it gets a little hot, your head is filled with a buzzing of flies;
If you go hungry, your body becomes as useless as a balky mule;
If you are tired, your own feet mock you.

That's another song the mountain people are singing as I write, while I hunt for a way to tell this story so that it will seem, at least, believable.

2
Which Is That of Suppositions

Introduction of the guests – An orator's trick – Posing the problem – Untenable hypotheses – The ultimate in absurdity – Non-Euclidean navigations in a dinner plate – Distinguished astronomers – How Mount Analogue exists just as if it did not exist – Light on the true history of the wizard Merlin – Of method in invention – The solar gate – Explanation of a geographic anomaly – The mid-point of land areas – A delicate calculation – The Redeemer of Millionaires – A poetic quitter – A friendly quitter – A pathetic quitter – A philosophic quitter – Precautions

The following Sunday at two in the afternoon I brought my wife to the 'laboratory' in the Passage des Patriarches. After half an hour the three of us formed a group for which the impossible no longer existed.

Father Sogol had just about finished his mysterious calculations, but he put off his account of them until a little later when everyone would be present. Meanwhile we decided to exchange descriptions of the people we had invited.

My guests were as follows:

Ivan Lapse, about thirty-five to forty, a Russian of Finnish birth and a remarkable linguist. Especially outstanding as a linguist because of his capacity to express himself orally or in writing with simplicity, elegance and precision in three or four different languages. Author of *The Tongue of Tongues* and of *Comparative Grammar of Gesture Languages*. A small, pale man with an elongated head – bald on top and fringed with black hair – long slanted black eyes, a thin nose, a clean-shaven face, and a slightly sad mouth. An excellent glacier climber, he had a particular liking for bivouacs at high altitudes.

Alphonse Camard, French, fifty, an esteemed and prolific poet, bearded, corpulent, with a lethargic manner a little like Verlaine's, redeemed by a fine warm voice. A liver complaint kept him out of long ascents, and he consoled himself by writing lovely poems on mountain themes.

Emile Gorge, French, twenty-five, a newspaperman, with a persuasive manner and a passion for music and choreography, about which he wrote brilliantly. A virtuoso of the *rappel de corde,* who preferred the descent to the ascent. Small, bizarrely built, with a thin body and a chubby face, having thick lips and not much chin.

Judith Pancake, an American friend of my wife's, around thirty, a mountain painter. Moreover, she is the only true painter of high mountains that I know. She understands that the view one has from a high peak is not registered in the same perceptive range as a still life or an ordinary landscape. Her paintings admirably express the circular structure of space in the upper regions. She does not consider herself an artist. She paints simply to 'have a souvenir' of her ascents. But she does it in such a workmanlike manner that her pictures, with their curved perspective, vividly recall those frescoes in which the old religious painters tried to represent the concentric circles of the celestial universe.

Father Sogol gave this description of his guests:

Arthur Beaver, forty-five to fifty, a physician, yachtsman, and mountain climber, and English of course; knows the Latin names, habits, and properties of all animals and plants on all the high mountain ranges of the earth. Is really happy only above an altitude of fifteen thousand feet. He forbade me to reveal how long and by what means he stayed at the summit of one of the Himalayas, because, as he said, as a doctor, gentleman, and true alpinist, he avoided fame like the plague. He had a large bony body, silvery-blond hair lighter than his tanned face, eyebrows perched very high, and finely drawn lips that hovered between naiveté and irony.

Two brothers, *Hans* and *Karl* (no one ever used their surname), about twenty-five and twenty-eight respectively. Austrians,

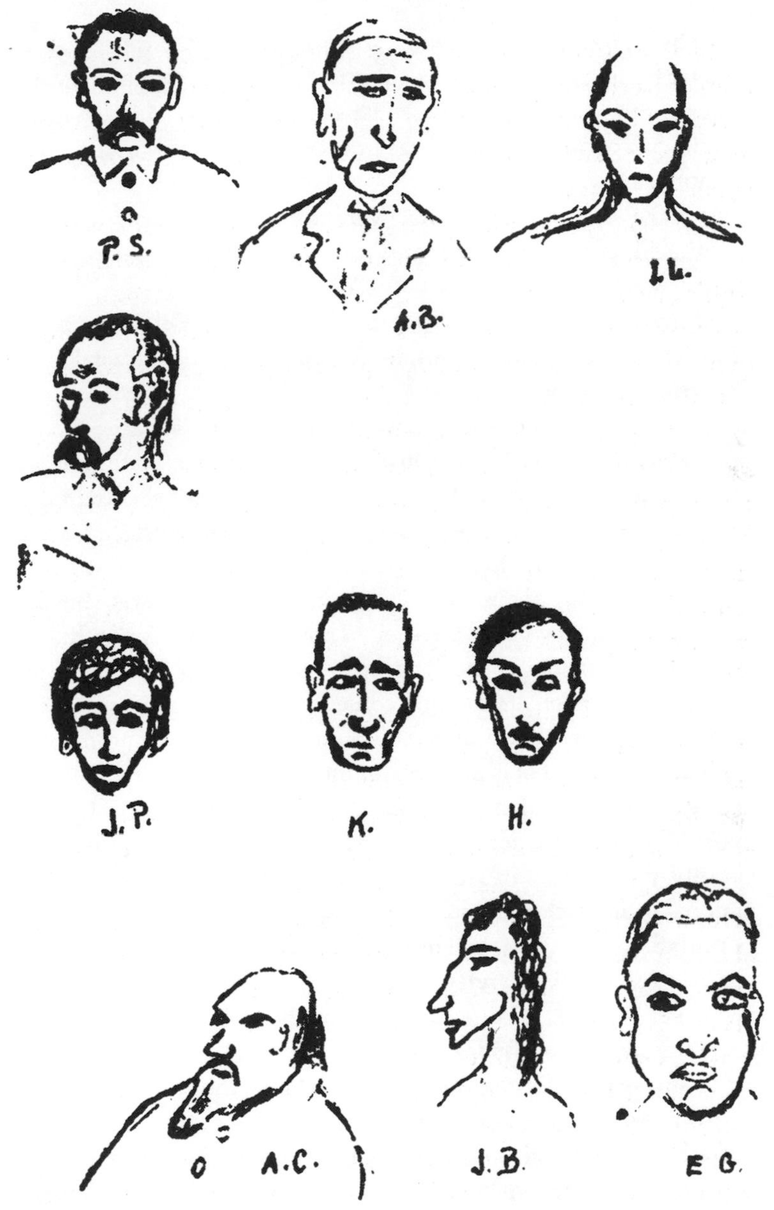
P. S.
A.B.
L.L.
J. P.
K.
H.
A.C.
J. B.
E G.

specialists in acrobatic climbing. Both blond, but the former with an oval head, the latter with a squarish look. Superbly built, with fingers of steel and eagle eyes. Hans was studying mathematical physics and astronomy. Karl was interested principally in Oriental metaphysics.

Arthur Beaver, Hans and Karl were the three friends Sogol had mentioned as forming with him an inseparable mountaineering team.

Julie Bonasse, between twenty-five and thirty, a Belgian actress. She was having just then a considerable success on the stage in Paris, Brussels, and Geneva. She was the confidante of a swarm of odd young people whom she guided into paths of sublime high-mindedness. She said, 'I adore Ibsen', and 'I adore chocolate éclairs', in the same tone of mouth-watering conviction. She believed in the existence of the 'fairy of the glaciers', and in winter she skied a great deal on slopes with cable lifts.

Benito Cicoria, about thirty, a ladies' tailor in Paris. Small, stylish, and a devotee of Hegel. Though Italian by birth, he belonged to a school of mountain climbing roughly designated as the German school. Its method could be described this way: You attack the steepest slope of a mountain along the least promising approach, the one that is most crumbling and exposed to rock slides, and you climb straight towards the summit without allowing yourself to look for any convenient detours to right or to left. Usually you succeed in killing yourself, but sooner or later some national team reaches the summit alive.

With Sogol, my wife, and me, it made twelve people all told.

The guests arrived pretty much on time. That is, the meeting being set for four o'clock, Dr Beaver showed up first at three fifty-nine, and Julie Bonasse, delayed by a rehearsal and last to arrive, made her entrance on the stroke of four thirty.

After the hubbub of introductions we all sat down at a large makeshift table, and our host began to speak. He repeated the general lines of the conversation he had had with me, reaffirmed his conviction about the existence of Mount Analogue, and announced he was going to organize an expedition to explore it.

'Most of you,' he went on, 'already know how I have been able to limit the area of investigation in a first approximation. But one or two of you are not yet informed. For you, and to refresh everyone's memory, I'll go over my calculations again.'

At that point he gave me a roguish and forceful look demanding my complicity in this adroit falsehood. For naturally everyone was still in the dark. But by this simple ruse each person had the impression of belonging to a minority, of being among 'one or two not yet informed', felt himself surrounded by a convinced majority, and was eager to be quickly convinced himself. This simple method of Sogol's for 'getting the audience into the palm of his hand', as he phrased it, was a simple application of the mathematical method that consists in 'considering the problem as solved'. And he also used the chemical analogy of a 'chain reaction'. But if this ruse was employed in the service of truth, could one still call it falsehood? In any case everyone pricked up his ears.

'I'll sum up the premises', he said. 'Firstly, Mount Analogue must be much higher than the highest mountains known today. Its summit must be inaccessible by means known up to now. But secondly, its base must be accessible to us, and its lower slopes must already be inhabited by human beings similar to us, for it is the path which links our present human domain to higher spheres. Inhabited, and therefore habitable. Therefore characterized by a set of conditions including climate, flora and fauna, and cosmic influences of all sorts not too different from the environment of our own continents. Since the mountain itself is extremely high, its base must be fairly broad; we are dealing with an area at least as large as that of the earth's largest islands – New Guinea, Borneo, Madagascar, perhaps even Australia.

'If we agree to this much, three questions arise: How has this territory thus far escaped the notice of explorers and travellers? How does one gain access to it? Where is it?

'The first question appears to be the most difficult to answer. How can it be that there exists on our earth a mountain higher than the highest peaks of the Himalayas, and that no one has as yet observed it? However, we know, a priori, by virtue of the laws of analogy, that it must exist. To explain why no one has yet observed it, several hypotheses can be offered. First, it may be located on the continent of the South Pole, which is still little known. But by taking a map of the points already reached on this continent and calculating through a simple geometrical construction the space which the human eye can embrace from these points, you can demonstrate that no elevation of more than twenty-five thousand feet could have gone unnoticed – no more in this region than in any other part of the planet.'

This argument struck me as being based on pretty debatable geography. But fortunately no one noticed. He went on.

'Are we dealing with a subterranean mountain then? Certain

legends, which have been handed down principally in Mongolia and Tibet, allude to an underground mountain, the seat of the ''King of the World'', where the ancient knowledge is preserved like an unperishing seed. But this realm does not correspond to the second condition of the mountain's existence; it could not afford a biological environment sufficiently close to ours; and even if this underground world exists, it is probably located beneath the slopes of Mount Analogue. All hypotheses of this order being inadmissible, we have to put the problem differently. The area we seek must be able to *exist in any region whatsoever* of the earth's surface. Therefore we must examine under what conditions it remains inaccessible not only to ships, airplanes and other vehicles but even to eyesight. I mean that it could perfectly well exist, *theoretically*, in the middle of this table, without our having the least suspicion it was there.

'To make myself understood, let me demonstrate an analogous case.'

He brought in from the next room a plate, which he placed on the table and into which he poured some oil. Then he tore up a piece of paper into tiny fragments, which he tossed on the surface of the oil.

'I have used oil because its high viscosity allows me to demonstrate my point more easily than with water, for example. Assume the surface of the oil is the surface of the earth; this piece of paper, a continent; this smaller piece, a ship. With the point of this needle, I'll push the ship gently towards the continent. You see that I can't make it touch or overlap. When it comes within a few millimetres of the shore, it seems to be repelled by a ring of oil enclosing the continent. Of course, by pushing a little harder, I can make them touch. But if the surface tension of the liquid were great enough, my ship could sail right around the continent without touching it. Now suppose that this invisible structure around the continent repels not only so-called material bodies but light rays as well. The navigator aboard the ship will sail around it not only without touching it but without even seeing it.

'The analogy becomes a bit too crude now, so let's put it aside. However, I imagine you know that a body does in fact exercise a repellent action of this kind on rays of light which pass close to it. This fact, predicted by Einstein, was verified by the astronomers Eddington and Crommelin on 30 March 1919, during a solar eclipse. They established that a star can be still visible even when, in relation to us, it has passed behind the solar disk. Doubtless this deviation is minute. But may there not exist unknown substances – unknown for this very reason in fact – capable of creating around them a much stronger *curvature of space*? It must be so, for it is the only possible explanation for our ignorance of the existence of Mount Analogue down to the present day.

'This, then, is what I have established simply by eliminating the untenable hypotheses. Somewhere on the Earth there exists an area with a circumference of at least several thousand kilometres and out of which Mount Analogue rises. The substrata of this territory are composed of materials which have the property of inducing curvature in such a way that the region is encased in a "shell" of curved space. Where do these materials come from? Are they of extra-terrestrial origin? Do they come from the interior of the earth, a region of whose physical nature we know so little that geologists are reduced to admitting that no substance can exist there either in the solid or in the liquid or in the gaseous state? I don't know, but we shall find out sooner or later when we are actually on the spot. I can further deduce that this shell cannot be completely closed; it must be open above in order to receive radiations of all kinds from the stars, essential to the life of *ordinary* man; it must also encompass a considerable portion of the earth's mass and doubtless opens towards its centre for similar reasons.'

He got up to sketch a little drawing on the blackboard.

'We can draw a diagram of the area something like this. These broken lines I'm making show the path of light rays. You see that these directional lines spread out in the sky, where they rejoin the general space structure of our cosmos. This opening out must take

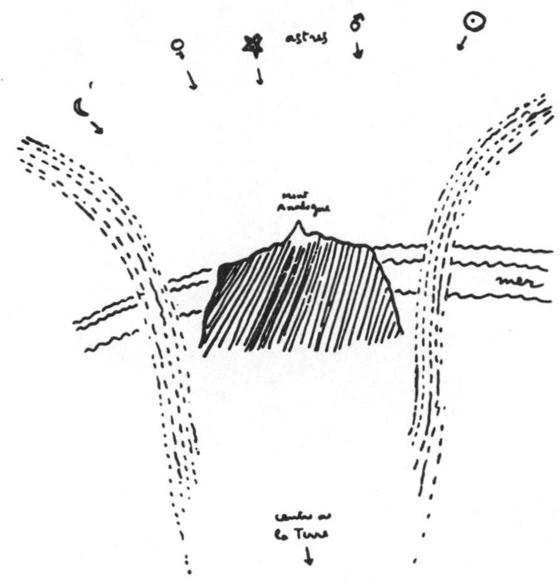

place at so great an altitude – far greater than the depth of our atmosphere – that it would be no use trying to enter the "shell" over the top in an airplane or balloon.

'If we visualize the area horizontally, we have this drawing. Remember that the immediate vicinity of Mount Analogue cannot present any noticeable spatial anomaly, since beings like ourselves must be able to exist there. It's a matter of a closed *ring of curvature*, spacious and impenetrable, which surrounds the country at a fixed distance with an invisible, intangible rampart. Because of it, *everything takes place as if Mount Analogue did not exist*. Supposing (in a minute I'll tell you why) the area in question is an island, here's how I'd have to draw the course of a ship going from *A* to *B*. Let's say we're aboard that ship. There's a lighthouse here at *B*. From *A* I point a glass straight ahead in line with the ship's course; I see the lighthouse at *B*, whose light has made a detour around the side of the mountain, and I will never suspect that between the light and me lies

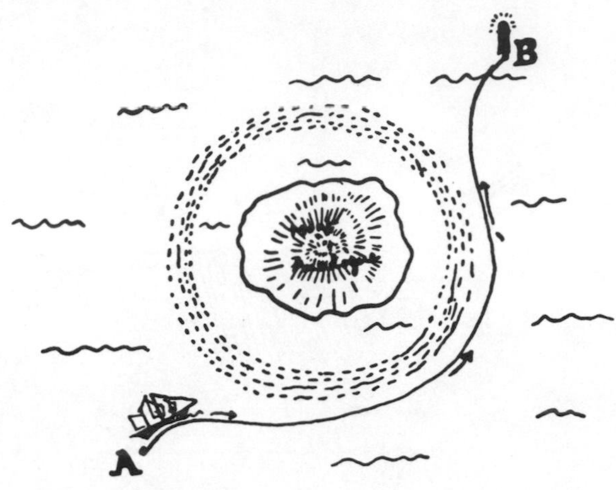

an island covered with high mountains. I continue on course. The curvature of space deflects the light from the stars and also the lines of force in the earth's magnetic field, so that in navigating with sextant and compass, I assume I am moving in a straight line. Without the rudder moving in the slightest, my ship and everything on board will be subject to the curvature and follow the contour deviation I have shown in the drawing between *A* and *B*. So even if this island is as big as Australia, it's understandable now that no one has ever suspected its existence. You see?'

Miss Pancake suddenly became pale with excitement.

'But that's exactly the story of Merlin in his magic circle. To tell the truth, I've always been convinced that the stupid business with Vivian was invented later by allegory hunters who missed the point. It was just part of his nature to hide inside his invisible circle, which could be anywhere.'

Sogol was quiet for a few moments to show how much he thought this comment was to the point.

'All right,' Dr Beaver said. 'But one day your captain is going to notice that he has burned more coal going from *A* to *B* than he should have.'

'Not at all, for in following the curvature of space, the ship itself lengthens proportionately to the curve; it's a matter of mathematics. The engines grow larger; each piece of coal stretches out . . .'

'Oh! I understand. In effect everything cancels out. But then how will anyone ever be able to land on the island, supposing we could determine its geographic position?'

'That was the second question to solve. I succeeded by following the same method, which consists in regarding the problem as solved and deducing from the solution all logical consequences. This method, by the way, has always served me well in every field.

'To find a way of reaching the island, one must assume the possibility and even the *necessity* of reaching it. The only admissible hypothesis is that the "shell of curvature" which surrounds the island is not absolutely impenetrable – that is, not *always*, not *everywhere*, and not *for everyone*. At a *certain moment* and in a *certain place certain persons* (those who know how and wish to do so) can enter. The privileged moment we're seeking must be determined by a standard unit of time common to Mount Analogue and to the rest of the world – therefore by a natural timepiece, very probably the course of the sun. This hypothesis is strongly supported by certain analogous considerations, and it is confirmed by the fact that it resolves another difficulty. Look back at my first drawing here. You notice how the lines of curvature rise and spread out high up in space. But in that case how could the sun send its rays down on the island from every point in its course? We are forced to the conclusion that the sun has the property of "uncurving" the space which surrounds the island. At sunrise and at sunset it must in some way penetrate the shell, and through that same breach we shall enter!'

We all sat stunned by the audacity and logical power of this deduction. Everyone kept silent, and everyone was convinced.

'A few *theoretical* points still remain obscure to me,' Sogol went on. 'I cannot claim to understand perfectly the relation between the sun and Mount Analogue. But *in practical application* there can be no doubt. We have only to take up our position in line with the sunrise or sunset (exactly to the east or to the west if it is at the solstice) and to await the proper moment. Then, for just a few minutes – as long as the solar disk remains on the horizon – the door will open, and I repeat, we shall enter.

'It's already late. I'll explain some other time (during the journey perhaps) why it is from the west and not from the east that it is possible to enter: It's both for a symbolic reason and because of the wind. We now have to examine the third question: Where is the island situated?

'Let's go on following the same method. A mass of heavy materials like Mount Analogue and its substructure would have to produce perceptible irregularities in the earth's motion – more extensive, according to my calculations, than the minor deviations observed to date. However, this mass exists. Therefore this invisible anomaly of the earth's surface must be compensated by some other anomaly. Now, we're lucky enough that the other anomaly is visible – so visible, even, that it has been obvious to geologists and geographers for a long time. It is simply the bizarre apportioning of dry land and sea, which divides our globe more or less into a "hemisphere of land masses" and a "hemisphere of oceans".'

He took a globe from the bookshelf and placed it on the table.

'I calculated as follows. First I draw this parallel, between fifty and fifty-two of north latitude; it is the one which traverses the longest stretch of dry land. Its runs across the southern part of Canada and then across the entire Eurasian continent from southern England to the island of Sakhalin. Now I draw in the meridian which crosses the longest stretch of dry land. It is located between twenty and twenty-eight of east longitude and runs through the Old World approximately from Spitzbergen to South Africa. I leave this margin of eight degrees because one can count the Mediterranean either as a true ocean or as a simple maritime pocket within the continent. According to certain traditions this meridian should pass

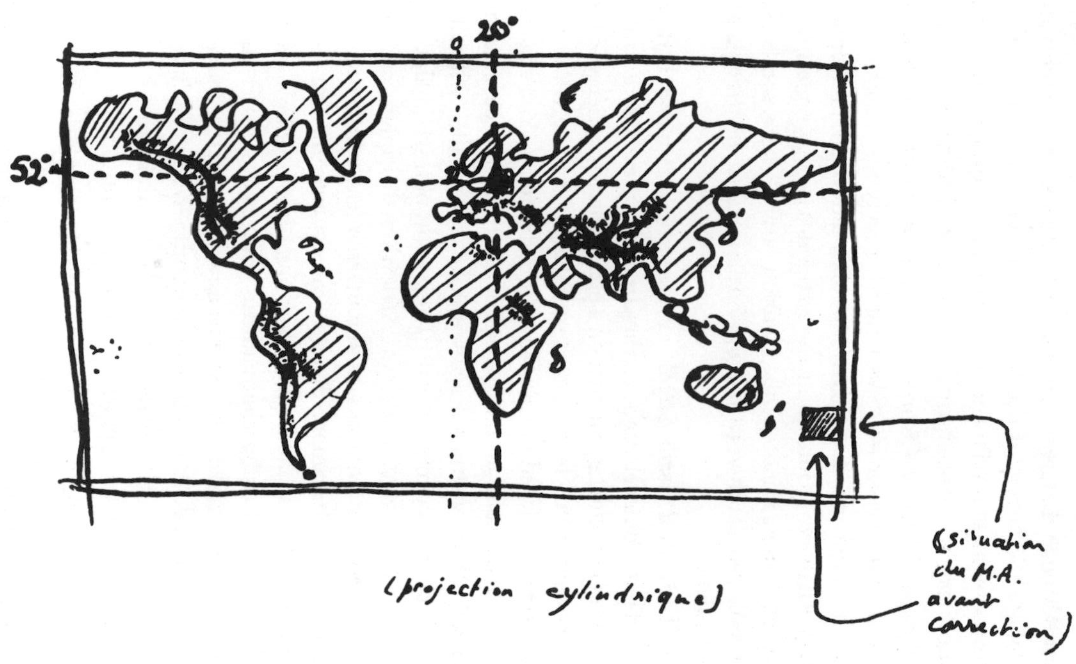

(projection cylindrique)

exactly through the Great Pyramids of Cheops. The principle hardly matters. The junction of the two lines, as you can see, takes place somewhere in eastern Poland or in the Ukraine or in White Russia, within the quadrilateral formed by Warsaw-Krakow-Minsk-Kiev.'

'Wonderful!' cried Cicoria, the Hegelian tailor. 'I follow you now. Since the island we're looking for surely has an area greater than that of the quadrilateral, the approximation does well enough. Mount Analogue is located at the antipodes of this region, which puts it . . . wait a minute while I work it out . . . here, southeast of Tasmania and southwest of New Zealand, west of the island of Auckland.'

'Well-reasoned,' said Sogol. 'Well-reasoned, but a little too hasty. That would be right if the dry land areas had a uniform thickness. But let's suppose that on a planisphere in relief we cut out the arrangement of land masses and suspended the whole thing from a string attached in this central quadrilateral. You can see at once that the great mountain masses in America, Eurasia and Africa, almost all of them situated below the fiftieth parallel, will tilt the planisphere heavily to the south. The weight of the Himalayas, the mountains of Mongolia and the African chains might even outweigh the American mountains and make it lean a little to the east. I'll know only after more detailed calculations. In any case the centre of gravity of the land masses must be moved considerably towards the south and perhaps a little towards the east. That could carry us into the Balkans or even to Egypt or towards Chaldea, the ancient biblical Eden . . . but let's not jump to any conclusions. In any case Mount Analogue remains in the South Pacific. It will take me a few more days to put my calculations into final form. Then we'll need some time for preparations – both to organize the expedition and to allow each one of us to put his affairs in order for a long journey. I suggest we set the date of departure around the first of October; that gives us two months before leaving, and we would arrive in the South Pacific in November – in the spring.

'A number of secondary but important problems remain – for example, material resources for outfitting the expedition.'

Arthur Beaver spoke up quickly: 'My yacht, *The Impossible*, is a sound little ship and has been around the world. She'll take us there. As to money, we'll see to that together, but from now on I'm certain we'll find everything we need.'

'With those fine words, my dear Arthur,' said Father Sogol, 'you earn the right to the title of Redeemer of Millionaires. But we still have a lot of work ahead of us. Each of us will have to do his share. Let's have our next meeting next Sunday at two. I'll give you the final results of my calculations, and we'll draw up a plan of action.'

After that we had a glass or two together and smoked a cigarette; then, using the dormer window and the rope, each of us took his leave, lost in his own thoughts.

Not much happened the next week. Except for the arrival of a few letters, that is. First, a word from the melancholy poet Alphonse Camard, who, after careful consideration, regretted that his health did not permit him to accompany us. He still wanted to participate in the expedition in his own way, and so he sent me some 'Wayfaring Songs of Mountaineers', through which, he said, his 'thoughts would follow us in this magnificent adventure'. They were written in various moods and for all stages of mountain climbing. I shall quote the one I liked best – though doubtless if you have never known the small hardships in question, you will find it idiotic. *It is in fact idiotic*, but as they say, it takes all kinds to make a world.

THE LAY OF THE LUCKLESS MOUNTAINEERS

The tea tastes of aluminium;
Twelve sleeping-bags for thirty men –
Everyone snug as a smothered bug.
Then off before the cracking dawn,

Mount Analogue

Breathing air like razor blades,
Between deathly black and deathly white.
My watch had the sense to stop;
Yours has gone on a spree.
We're smeared to the elbows with honey;
The sky's all curds and whey.
It's light before we get going,
The névé's already turned yellow,
It's already raining pebbles,
And the cold seeps into your hands.
Who put gasoline in the drinking water?
Our fingers swell like sponges,
And the rope feels like a telegraph pole.

The shelter's jumping with fleas;
Our snoring sounds like the Paris zoo.
My ear's cracking off from frostbite.
You look like a half-trussed duck.
I can never find enough pockets;
My compass went out with the prune pits.
Like a good boy scout I forgot my knife,
So pass me that folding sabre of yours.

We've been climbing for twenty-five thousand hours,
And we're not yet in sight of the lower slope.
All that chocolate has corked us tight.
You're slogging in cheese when you break through the glaze.
The cloud tastes like nitric acid,
And you stare two paces into solid white.

Hold up so we can set ourselves straight.
My knapsack's beating instead of my heart;
It skipped out way back for sea level.
And holes, what holes! Green going to black,
With gurgling sounds and chemins de fer.
Ten thousand pockets in the moraine,
False pockets, real holes, who knows?
What's a broken leg on a mountaintop?

Here's my schaos*; let's have your stew pan.*
We'll see it through on prudence and prunes.
Just wait till the glacier splits its sides;
They'll find us by our bushy beards.
Space itself has turned to sleet;
We've taken the wrong couloir *again.*
I can hear your knees from here, old man.
This rock ledge won't give up.
You know what I have? A memory block,
A stomach cramp, a flaming thirst,
And two fingers turned pale green.

We never did see the summit –
Except on the sardine can.
The rope jammed on every pull-through.
We passed a lifetime untangling the line
And came to our senses with the cows in the dell.

'Have a good climb?'
'First rate. But tough.'

I also received a letter from Emile Gorge, the newspaperman. He had promised to meet a friend in the Oisans in August and make the descent from the central peak of La Meije by the southern face – where a stone drops straight down for five or six seconds before touching bottom. After that he had a story to do in the Tyrol. He did not want us to delay our departure for his sake, and moreover, since he would be in Paris, he offered to place any accounts we wanted to send him of our voyage.

Sogol had received a long, moving letter, vibrant and pathetic, from Julie Bonasse, torn between the desire to accompany us and her devotion to her Art – it was the most cruel sacrifice that the jealous god of the Theatre had ever demanded of her . . . and she was almost prepared to rebel and follow her selfish inclinations. But what would then become of her dear little friends whose suffering souls she had taken under her care?

'Well?' Sogol inquired after reading me the letter. 'Doesn't that bring tears to your eyes? Are you so unfeeling that your heart won't melt? I was so deeply moved by the thought that she might still be in doubt that I replied immediately urging her to stay with her lost souls and high intentions.'

Benito Cicoria had written to him also. A careful examination of his letter, twelve pages all told, led us to the conclusion that he, too, had decided not to come along. His reasons were given in a series of superbly constructed 'dialectical triads'. It would be impossible to summarize them; one would have to follow the entire progression, a dangerous exercise in itself. I quote one sentence at random: 'Although the triad possible-impossible-adventure may be regarded as immediately phenomenizable and therefore as phenomenizing in respect to the first ontological trial, it is so only on the condition – in reality epistemological – of a dialectic *reversus* whose prediscursive content is no different from a *historical predisposition* implying the practical reversibility of the ontologically oriented process – an implication which only the *facts* can justify.' Of course, of course.

All in all, four fast fade-outs, as they say. That left eight of us. Sogol confided to me that he had expected a few to drop out. It is for just that reason that he had pretended at the meeting that his calculations were not finished, whereas in reality they were. He did not want the extra position of Mount Analogue to be known outside the members of the expedition. It will be apparent later on how wise his precautions were, and that they were insufficient even. If everything had conformed exactly to Sogol's deductions, if one aspect of the problem had not escaped him, this insufficiency of precautions would have led to horrible disaster.

3
Which Is That of the Crossing

Makeshift sailors – Lending a hand – Historical and psychological details – Measuring the power of human thought – How we can count up to four at the most – Complementary experiments – Provisions – A portable kitchen garden – Artificial symbiosis – Heating devices – The western approach and the ocean breeze – Gropings – Whether glaciers are living creatures – The Tale of the Hollow-Men and the Bitter-Rose – The money question

On the tenth of the following October we embarked aboard *The Impossible*. There were eight of us: Arthur Beaver, owner of the yacht; Pierre Sogol, head of the expedition; Ivan Lapse, the linguist; the brothers Hans and Karl; Judith Pancake, the painter of mountain heights; my wife; and I. We had agreed not to speak to our friends of the exact goal of our expedition, for either they would have thought us crazy, or, more probably, they would have believed we were inventing stories to hide the true purpose of our enterprise. There was no telling what they might imagine that to be. We had announced that we were going to explore a few South Sea islands, the mountains of Borneo, and the Australian Alps. Each of us had made arrangements for a prolonged absence from Europe.

Arthur Beaver had seen fit to warn his crew that the expedition would be long and might involve some risks. He discharged with compensation the men with families and kept only three old salts in addition to the 'Captain', an Irishman and a skilled navigator for whom *The Impossible* had become a second self. The eight of us decided to replace the missing crew, and moreover it would be the most interesting way to spend our time during the crossing.

We were by no means cut out to be sailors. Several of us were seasick. Others, who were never so much in command of their bodies as when hanging over an icy abyss, were nevertheless unnerved by the little ship's long slidings down the watery slopes. The path to our highest desires often lies through the undesirable.

The Impossible, a two-master, ran under sail whenever the wind was favourable. Hans and Karl came to understand the air, the wind and the canvas with their bodies, the way they understood rock slopes and the line. The two women performed endless miracles in the galley. Father Sogol helped the captain, took our bearings, assigned us our tasks, helped us get the knack of things, and kept an eye on odd details. Arthur Beaver swabbed down the deck and looked after our health. Ivan Lapse took over as engineer, and I made a passable stoker.

The demands of intensive communal work bound us together as if we had been a single family, and a pretty rare family at that. Still, the group contained an odd assortment of temperaments. To tell the truth, Ivan Lapse sometimes found that Miss Pancake was hopelessly devoid of any sense of proper word usage; Hans eyed me suspiciously whenever I presumed to speak of the so-called exact sciences and considered my remarks disrespectful; Karl was not happy working beside Sogol, who, he maintained, smelled like a Negro when he perspired; Dr Beaver's expression of contentment whenever he ate herring made me irritable. But dear old Beaver, as doctor and master of the ship, saw to it that no infection broke out in either the body or the spirit of the expedition. Whenever we began to get on each other's nerves because of someone's way of walking, talking, breathing or eating, he always showed up in time with an easy, chiding comment.

If I were to tell this story the way history is usually written or the way each of us recalls his own past, which means recording only the most glorious moments and inventing a new continuity for them, I should omit these little details and say that our eight stout hearts drummed from morning to night in time with a single all-encompassing desire – or some such lie. But the flame that kindles desire and illuminates thought never burned for more than a few seconds at a stretch. The rest of the time we tried to remember it.

Fortunately the demands of daily work, in which each of us had his vital role, reminded us that we had come aboard of our own free will, that we were indispensable to one another, and that we were on a ship – that is to say, in a temporary habitation, designed to transport us somewhere else. If anyone forgot it, someone else lost no time in reminding him.

In this connection Father Sogol had described to us some experiments he had done a few years before with the idea of measuring the power of human thought. I shall repeat only the parts I could grasp. At the time I wondered how literally one should take it all, and forever preoccupied with my favourite field of study, I admired Sogol as an inventor of 'abstract symbols' (in other words, an abstract thing symbolizing a concrete thing, the reverse of the normal order). But since then I have found that these notions of abstract and concrete have no great significance, as I should have learned reading Xenophon of Elis or even Shakespeare: a thing either is or is not, and that's the end of it. Well, Sogol had tried to 'measure thought'; not the way psychotechnicians and testing experts go at it, limiting themselves to comparing the way one individual performs a certain activity (often, moreover, entirely alien to thought) to the average performance of other individuals of the same age. He was intent on measuring the power of thought as an absolute value.

'This power,' Sogol said, 'is arithmetical. In reality every thought represents a capacity to grasp the divisions of a whole. Now, numbers are nothing else than the divisions of a unity, which is to say, *the divisions of any whole whatever*. In myself and in others I began to observe how many numbers a man really can conceive, that is to say, can carry in his mind without breaking them down or writing them out; how many successive consequences of a principle he can grasp at once, instantaneously; how many inclusions of species within genus; how many relations of cause to effect, of means to end. And I never found the number to be greater than four. And moreover, this figure four required an exceptional mental exertion which I obtained only rarely. The thought of an idiot stops at one, and the ordinary thought of most people goes to two, sometimes to three, very rarely to four. If you like, I'll summarize one or two of these experiments for you. Follow me carefully.'

To understand what follows, one must perform the proposed experiments in good faith. It requires considerable attention, patience, and serenity of mind.

He went on as follows:

'Represent to yourself simultaneously the following facts: 1. I get dressed to go out; 2. I go out to catch a train; 3. I catch the train to go to work; 4. I go to work to earn a living. Now try to add a fifth step, and I am sure that at least one of the first three will vanish from your mind.'

We performed the experiment; he was right, and even a little too generous.

'Take another type of sequence: 1. the spaniel is a dog; 2. dogs are mammals; 3. mammals are vertebrates; 4. vertebrates are animals . . . I'll carry it further: Animals are living creatures – but there, I've already forgotten the spaniel. If I recall the spaniel, I forget vertebrates . . . In any logical sequence of division or progression, you will run into the same phenomenon. That's why we're constantly mistaking accident for substance, effect for cause, means for end, our ship for a permanent habitation, our bodies or our minds for ourselves, and ourselves for something eternal.'

The hold of the little ship had been filled with various instruments and supplies. Beaver had studied the question of provisions methodically and imaginatively. Five tons of goods would have to feed all eight of us, plus the four crew members, for two years, without our relying on any fresh food found en route. The art of keeping well-fed is an important part of mountaineering, and the doctor had carried it to a high degree of perfection. Beaver had invented a 'portable kitchen garden' weighing no more than a pound. It was a mica box containing a synthetic earth in which he planted certain fast-growing seeds. Every other day each one of these devices produced a ration of green vegetables sufficient for one man – plus a few delicious mushrooms. He had also tried to exploit modern methods of tissue culture. Instead of raising cattle, he said to himself, why not raise beefsteaks directly? But his experiments had not advanced beyond the stage of requiring heavy and fragile equipment that produced a revolting slime, and he gave up the effort. We would do better going without meat.

With Hans's help, Beaver had, moreover, perfected the breathing and heating apparatus that he had used in the Himalayas. The respiratory mechanism was very ingenious. A mask of elastic material fitted over the face. Air was exhaled through a tube into the 'portable garden', where the chlorophyl of young plants, hyper-activated by the ultraviolet radiations of high altitude, absorbed the carbon out of the carbon dioxide and returned the oxygen to the man. The lung action and the elasticity of the mask maintained a slight compression, and the apparatus was set to keep the proper amount of carbon dioxide in the air inhaled. The plants also absorbed the excess of moisture exhaled, and the warmth of the breath activated their growth. Thus the animal-vegetable cycle functioned on an individual scale, a state that permitted a considerable economy of supplies. In brief, a kind of artificial symbiosis was achieved between animal and vegetable. Other nourishment was provided in the concentrated form of flour, solidified oil, sugar, dried milk and cheese.

For extreme altitudes we carried oxygen bottles and well-designed respiratory apparatus. When the time comes, I shall speak of the discussions we had over this equipment and of what happened to it.

Dr Beaver had also developed clothing that supplied heat by

internal catalytic combustion, but after experimentation he had determined that good eiderdown garments, lined with air pockets to hold body heat, are sufficient for walking in the severest cold. Heating devices are necessary only during bivouacs, and then one can keep warm with the same stoves used for cooking, fed by naphthalene. This easily packed substance furnishes intense heat from a small volume, provided it burns in a special stove guaranteeing complete (and therefore odourless) combustion. However, we did not know how high our exploration would take us, and as a precaution we had also brought along heating garments with double linings of platinized asbestos, into which was blown air saturated with alcohol fumes.

Naturally, we also carried all the standard mountain-climbing equipment: cleated shoes and nails of all kinds, ropes, screw rings, hammers, snap hooks, ice axes, crampons, snow-shoes, skis and all accessories, as well as instruments for observation like compasses, clinometers, altimeters, barometers, thermometers, range-finders, alidades and cameras. And arms: rifles, carbines, revolvers, short sabres, dynamite – in other words, enough to face any foreseeable obstacle.

Sogol kept the log himself. I am too little versed in nautical matters to speak of any minor incidents that may have affected our course. Navigation proceeded smoothly. After sailing from La Rochelle, we stopped at the Azores, Guadeloupe, Colon, and having passed through the Panama Canal, we entered the South Pacific during the first week of November.

It was on one of those days that Sogol explained to us why it was necessary to try to approach the invisible continent from the west, just at sundown, and not from the east at sunrise. It is because at that moment, as in Franklin's experiment with the heated chamber, a cool offshore breeze must blow in towards the overheated lower layers of the atmosphere of Mount Analogue. Thus we would be sucked in towards the interior, whereas at dawn and from the east we should be violently driven off. Furthermore this result was symbolically predictable. Civilizations, in their natural process of degeneration, move from east to west. To return to the source of things, one has to travel in the opposite direction.

Having once reached the region that should have been located just to the west of Mount Analogue, we had to grope around a little. We patrolled back and forth at half speed, and every evening just when the disk of the sun was about to touch the horizon, we took up a westerly heading and waited, barely breathing, our eyes staring, until the sun had disappeared. The ocean was always beautiful, but the suspense was wearing. Day after day went by that way, with a few minutes of hope and expectant curiosity each evening. Doubt and impatience began to show the tips of their ears among the company of *The Impossible*. Fortunately Sogol had warned us that these gropings would probably last a month or two.

We stuck it out. To fill the difficult hours after twilight, we often swapped stories.

I remember one night when we were talking about mountain legends. I said it seemed to me that mountainous regions were far less rich in fantastic legends than the sea or the great forests. Karl had an explanation of his own for that.

'At high altitudes,' he said, 'there's no place for the fantastic, because reality in itself is more marvellous than anything man could imagine. Could anyone dream up a gnome or a giant or a hydra or a catoblepas to rival the terrifying power and mystery of a glacier, the tiniest little glacier? For glaciers are living creatures; their substance renews itself in an unfailing periodic process.

'The glacier is an organized being, with a head or névé through which it gulps snow and rock debris, a head well separated from the rest of its body by the *rimaye*; then an enormous stomach in which snow is transformed into ice, a stomach riddled with crevasses and internal passages for expelling excess water; and in its lower portions it secretes its wastes in the form of moraine. Its life follows the cycle of the seasons. It sleeps in winter and comes to life in the spring with deep creakings and boomings. Certain glaciers even reproduce themselves, by means that are little more rudimentary than those of unicellular beings – either by conjunction and fusion or by division, which gives birth to what are called regenerate glaciers.'

'I suspect,' Hans replied, 'that what you're giving us there is a metaphysical definition of life, not a scientific one. Living beings nourish themselves by chemical means, whereas the mass of a glacier is maintained by physical and mechanical processes: freezing and melting, compression and churning.'

'That's all very true,' Karl answered. 'But you scientists who study crystallizable viruses, for example, in hopes of finding the transitional stages between the physical and the chemical and between the chemical and the biological, you could learn a great deal from observing glaciers. Perhaps nature made them in a first attempt to create living beings by exclusively physical processes.'

'Perhaps,' said Hans. '"Perhaps" has no meaning for me. What remains certain is that a glacier contains no carbon, and that therefore it cannot be an organic substance.'

Ivan Lapse, who liked to show off his knowledge of numerous literatures, interrupted: 'Either way, Karl is right about our reactions to mountains. Victor Hugo, coming down from the Rigi, which even in his day was not considered very high, remarked that the view of the world from high peaks does such violence to our visual habits that the natural takes on the appearance of the supernatural. He even asserted that the average human mind cannot bear such a wrenching of its perceptions, and that was his explanation for the large number of mental cases in mountainous country.'

'It's true, perfectly true,' said Arthur Beaver, 'even though that last theory is utter nonsense. Last night Miss Pancake showed me some sketches of mountain landscapes which confirm what you say . . .'

Miss Pancake upset her teacup and fidgeted nervously while Beaver went on:

'But you're wrong in saying that high altitudes are not rich in legends. I've heard some pretty weird ones. I'll admit it wasn't in Europe I heard them.'

'We're all ears,' Sogol said right away.

'Not tonight,' Beaver answered. 'I'd be happy to tell you one of those stories, even though the people who told it to me made me promise not to reveal its origin, and besides, that hardly matters. But I'd like to tell it as faithfully as possible. To do that I'll have to reconstruct it in the original language and get our friend Lapse to help me translate it. Tomorrow afternoon, if you like, I'll let you hear it.'

The next day after lunch, since the yacht was becalmed on a flat sea, we gathered around to hear the story. Usually we spoke English among us and sometimes French, for everyone could follow in both languages. Ivan Lapse had preferred to translate the legend into French, and he read it himself.

The Tale of the Hollow-Men and the Bitter-Rose

The Hollow-Men live in solid rock and move about in it in the form of mobile caves or recesses. In ice they appear as bubbles in the shape of men. But they never venture out into the air, for the wind would blow them away.

They have houses in the rock whose walls are made of emptiness, and tents in the ice whose fabric is of bubbles. During the day they stay in the stone, and at night they wander through the ice and dance during the full moon. But they never see the sun, or else they would burst.

They eat only the void, such as the form of corpses; they get drunk on empty words and all the meaningless expressions we utter.

Some people say they have always existed and will exist forever. Others say they are the dead. And others say that as a sword has its scabbard or a foot its imprint, every living man has in the mountain his Hollow-Man, and in death they are reunited.

In the village of Hundred-Houses there lived the old priest-magician Hunoes and his wife, Hulay-Hulay. They had two sons, two identical twins who could not be told apart, called Mo and Ho. Even their mother got them mixed up. To tell them apart on the day of name-giving, they had put on Mo a necklace bearing a little cross and on Ho a necklace bearing a little ring.

Old Hunoes had one great unconfessed worry. According to custom his elder son should succeed him. But which was his elder son? Did he even have an elder son?

At the age of adolescence Mo and Ho were already accomplished mountaineers. They came to be called the two mountain goats. One day, their father told them, 'To whichever one of you brings back to me the Bitter-Rose I shall hand on the great knowledge.'

The Bitter-Rose is found only at the summit of the highest peaks. Whoever eats of it finds that whenever he is about to tell a lie, aloud or to himself, his tongue begins to burn. He can still tell falsehoods, but he has been warned. A few people have seen the Bitter-Rose: According to what they say, it looks like a large multi-coloured lichen or a swarm of butterflies. But no one has ever been able to pick it, for the tiniest tremor of fear anywhere close by alerts it, and it disappears into the rock. Even if one desires it, one is a little afraid of possessing it, and it vanishes.

To describe an impossible action or an absurd undertaking, they say: 'It's like looking for night in broad daylight,' or 'It's like wanting to throw light on the sun in order to see it better,' or 'It's like trying to catch the Bitter-Rose.'

Mo has taken his ropes and pick and hatchet and iron hooks. At sunrise he is already high up on a peak called Cloudy Head. Like a lizard, sometimes like a spider, he inches upward across the high red precipice, between white snow below and the blue-black sky. Little swift-moving clouds envelop him from time to time and then expose him suddenly to the light again. And now at last, a little distance above him, he sees the Bitter-Rose, shimmering with unearthly tints. He repeats to himself unceasingly the charm that his father has taught him to ward off fear.

He's going to need a screw ring here, with a rope sling, in order to straddle this outcropping of rock like a rearing horse. He strikes with his hammer, and his hand breaks through into a hole. There is a hollow under the stone. Shattering the crust around it, he sees that the hollow is in the form of a man: torso, legs, arms, and little tubes in the shape of fingers spread in terror. He has split the head with the blow of his pick.

An icy wind passes across the stone. Mo has killed a Hollow-Man. He has shuddered, and the Bitter-Rose has retreated into the rock.

Mo climbs back down to the village and tells his father, 'I killed a Hollow-Man. But I saw the Bitter-Rose, and tomorrow I shall go to look for it.'

Old Hunoes became grave. Far off he saw one misfortune after another coming in procession. He said: 'Watch out for the Hollow-Men. They will seek vengeance. They cannot enter our world, but they can come up to the surface of things. Beware of the surface of things.'

At dawn the next day Hulay-Hulay gave a great cry, rose up, and ran towards the mountain. At the foot of the red cliff lay Mo's garments, his ropes and hatchet, and his medal with the cross. His body was no longer there.

'Ho,' she cried, running back. 'They've killed your brother. They've killed my son.'

Ho rises up with his teeth clenched and the skin tightening on his scalp. He takes his hatchet and prepares to set out. His father says to him: 'First, listen to me. This is what you have to do. The Hollow-Men have taken your brother and changed him into a Hollow-Man. He will try to escape. He will go in search of light to the seracs of the Clear Glacier. Put his medal around your neck as well as your own. Go to him and strike at his head. Enter the form of his body, and Mo will live again among us. Do not fear to kill a dead man.'

Ho gazes wide-eyed into the blue ice of the Clear Glacier. Is the light playing tricks on him, are his eyes deceiving him, or is he really seeing what he sees? He watches silvery forms with arms and legs, like greased divers under water. There is his brother, Mo, his hollow shape fleeing from a thousand Hollow-Men in pursuit. But they are afraid of the light. Mo's form seeks the light and rises in a large blue serac, turning around and around as if in search of a door. Despite his bursting heart and the blood clotting in his veins, Ho steps forward. To his blood and to his heart he says, 'Do not fear to kill a dead man.' Then he strikes the head, shattering the ice. Mo's form becomes motionless; Ho opens the ice of the serac and enters his brother's form like a sword fitted into its sheath, a foot into its imprint. He moves his elbows and works himself into place, then draws his legs back out of the mould of ice. And he hears himself saying words in a language he had never spoken. He feels he is Ho, and that he is Mo at the same time. All Mo's memories have entered his mind – the way up Cloudy Head and where the Bitter-Rose has its habitation.

With the circle and the cross around his neck, he comes to Hulay-Hulay. 'Mother, you will have no more trouble telling us apart. Mo and Ho are now in the same body; I am your only son, Moho.'

Old Hunoes shed a few tears, and his face showed happiness. But there was still one doubt he wished to dispel. He said to Moho, 'You are my only son; Ho and Mo can no longer be distinguished.'

Moho told him with conviction, 'Now I can reach the Bitter-Rose. Mo knows the way; Ho knows the right gesture. Master of my fears, I shall have the flower of discernment.'

He picked the flower, he received the teaching, and old Hunoes was able to leave this world peacefully.

That evening the sun went down once again without opening the door of another world for us.

Another question had preoccupied us a great deal during those days of waiting. You do not set out to acquire something in a foreign country without a supply of money. For purposes of barter with such 'savages' and 'natives' as they meet, explorers usually carry with them all sorts of knick-knacks and junk – knives, mirrors, Paris souvenirs, inventors' leftovers, braces, patent sock-suspenders, trinkets, cretonne, pieces of soap, eau-de-vie, old rifles, harmless ammunition, saccharin, caps, combs, tobacco, pipes, medals and cord – not to speak of devotional objects. Since we might, during the course of the voyage and even in the interior of the continent, meet peoples belonging to ordinary humanity, we had provided ourselves with such wares. But in our relations with the superior beings of Mount Analogue, what would be suitable for barter? What did we possess of real value? With what could we pay for the new knowledge we were seeking? Would we have to accept it as charity or on credit?

Each one of us kept making his personal inventory, and each one of us felt poorer as the days went on. For no one saw anything around him or in him which really belonged to him. It reached the point where we were just eight beggars, possessing nothing, who each night watched the sun sink toward the horizon.

4

In Which We Arrive and in Which the Problem of Money Arises in Precise Terms

Here we are – Everything novel, nothing astonishing – Interrogation – Going ashore in Port o' Monkeys – The old ships – The monetary system – The peradam, standard of all value – The resigned residents of the coast – Settling of the colonies – Fascinating pastimes – Metaphysics, sociology, linguistics – Flora, fauna, myths – Plans for exploration and study – 'When are you getting under way?' – A nasty owl – Unexpected rain – Simplifying our equipment, exterior and interior – The first peradam!

Long expectation of the unknown lessens the final effect of surprise. Here we are, settled only three days in our little temporary house in Port o' Monkeys on the slopes of Mount Analogue, and everything already has a familiar air. Out of my window I can see *The Impossible* anchored in a creek, and the bay that opens out to a horizon just like all ocean horizons, except that it rises perceptibly from dawn to noon following the sun, then sinks from noon to dusk, by an optical phenomenon Sogol is racking his brains to figure out in the next room. Since I have been entrusted with keeping the log of the expedition, I have been trying since this morning to put down on paper the circumstances of our arrival on the continent. I do not know how to describe that impression of something at the same time quite extraordinary and entirely familiar, that giddy, bewildering sensation of having been here before. I have tried to use the personal notes jotted down by my companions, and they will help a little. I was also counting on the photographs and movies that Hans and

Karl took; but after developing, no image at all appeared on the films. We were unable to photograph anything here with ordinary equipment – another optical problem for Sogol to rack his brains over.

Three days ago, then, just as the sun was going to disappear again over the horizon, while we waited tense in the bows with the sun behind us, a wind arose without any warning, or rather a powerful suction suddenly pulled us forward, space opened ahead of us, a bottomless emptiness, a horizontal abyss of air and water impossibly entwined. The boat creaked in all its timbers and was hurled forward unerringly along a rising slope as far as the centre of the abyss and was suddenly set adrift in a wide calm bay, in sight of land! The shore was near enough for us to make out trees and houses and, higher up, cultivated fields, forests, meadows, rocks, and higher still, row after row of tall peaks and glaciers flaming scarlet in the setting sun. A flotilla of boats each manned by ten oarsmen – clearly Europeans, with naked and browned torsos – came out to tow us in to an anchorage. It certainly seemed as though we were expected. The place looked very much like a Mediterranean fishing village. We did not feel lost or out of place. The leader of the flotilla led us in silence to a white house, into a bare room with a red tile floor, where a man in mountain dress received us on a carpet. He spoke perfect French, but with the inward smile of someone who feels the strangeness of the expressions he must use to make himself understood. He was translating, without hesitation or incorrectness, but obviously translating.

He questioned us one after the other. Each one of his questions – all of them very simple: Who were we? Why had we come? – caught us completely off our guard and seemed to probe our very insides. Who are you? Who am I? We could not answer him as we would a police official or a customs inspector. Give one's name and profession? What does that mean? But *who* are you? And *what* are you? The words we uttered – we had none better – were worthless, repugnant and grotesque as dead things. We realized that with the guides of Mount Analogue, we could no longer get away with just words. Sogol courageously took it upon himself to give a brief account of our voyage.

The man receiving us was indeed a guide. All authority in this country is exercised by the mountain guides, who form a distinct class and, outside their work as guides, assume in rotation the essential administrative functions in the villages of the coast and the lower slopes. This man gave us pertinent information on the country and on what we were expected to do. We had come ashore in a little coastal town peopled by Europeans, for the most part French. There are no natives here. All inhabitants have come from elsewhere, from the four corners of the world like ourselves, and each nation has its little colony along the shore. How did it happen that we had fallen precisely on this town, Port o' Monkeys, peopled by western Europeans? We were to learn later that it was not by chance, and that the wind that had carried us there was no natural and fortuitous wind but had blown in accordance with a will. And why this name, Port o' Monkeys, when there was not a single quadrumanous species in the region? I find it hard to describe my reaction, but that name summoned up in my mind, rather disagreeably, all my heritage as a twentieth-century Occidental – something curious, imitative, shameless, agitated. Our port of arrival could not have been any other than Port o' Monkeys. From here, by our own devices, we would have to reach the chalets at the base, two days' journey away in the upper pastures, where we would meet the guide who could lead us higher. We should therefore have to stay a few days in Port o' Monkeys to prepare our baggage and organize a caravan of porters, for we had to carry up to the base enough supplies for a very long stay. We were taken to a little house, very clean and sparsely furnished. Each of us had a kind of cell that he could arrange as he pleased, and there was a large central room with a fireplace where we gathered for meals and for the evening council.

Behind the house a snowy peak peered at us over its wooded

shoulder. In front stretched the harbour where our ship lay, the last arrival in the strangest fleet one could imagine. In the inlets along the shore, ships of all epochs and all nations were lined up in uneven ranks, the oldest so encrusted with salt and algae and shells as to be no longer recognizable. There were Phoenician barks, triremes, galleys, caravels, schooners; along with two paddle steamers and an old wood and steel sloop from the last century. But there were very few ships of recent date. We could rarely identify the most ancient ones with a name or a country. And all these abandoned hulks calmly awaited petrification or slow consumption by marine flora and fauna, the disintegration and dispersion of matter which await all inert objects, even if they have served the highest purposes.

The first two days were spent transporting the cargo of provisions and equipment from the yacht to our house, checking the condition of everything, and preparing the loads we would have to carry up to the chalets at the base in two stages and several trips. With the help of the captain and the three sailors, the eight of us accomplished all this fairly quickly. For the first stage of the journey, which would take a day, there was a good trail and we would be able to use the sturdy brown donkeys of the country. From there on, everything had to be carried by men. So we had to rent donkeys and hire porters. The money problem, which had troubled us so much, had been at least provisionally solved on our arrival. The guide who received us had handed over to us, as an advance, a sack of the metal tokens that serve as currency to exchange for goods and services. As we had foreseen, none of our money had any value. Each new arrival or group of arrivals receives this form of advance to cover initial expenses; it is understood that one will pay it back in the course of one's stay on the continent of Mount Analogue. But how can one pay back the tokens? There are several ways, and since this question of exchange and reimbursement forms the basis of all human existence and social life in the settlements along the coast, I shall have to add a few details.

There is found here, rarely on the lower slopes and more

frequently as one ascends, a clear and extremely hard stone, spherical and of variable size. It is a true crystal and – an extraordinary instance entirely unknown elsewhere on this planet – a curved crystal. In the French spoken in Port o' Monkeys, this stone is called *peradam*. Ivan Lapse is still puzzled by the formation and the root meaning of the word. It may mean, as he sees it, 'harder than diamond', as is very much the case, or else 'father of diamond'. And some say that diamond is in reality the product of the disintegration of peradam by a sort of squaring of the circle or, more exactly, cubing of the sphere. Or else the word may mean 'Adam's stone' and have had some secret and profound complicity with the original nature of man. This stone is so perfectly transparent and its index of refraction so close to that of air in spite of the crystal's great density that the inexperienced eye barely perceives it. But to any person who seeks it with sincerity and out of true need it reveals itself by a brilliant sparkle like that of a dewdrop. Peradam is the only substance, the only material thing, whose value is recognized by the guides of Mount Analogue. Therefore it remains the basis and standard of all currency, like gold in many countries.

The only true means of repaying one's debt in full is in peradams. But peradams are rare; the search for them is difficult and even dangerous, for it is often necessary to extract one from a fissure in the face of a precipice or to pry one out of a sloping overhang of ice where it has embedded itself on the very lip of a crevasse. Therefore, after efforts that sometimes last years, many people become discouraged and go back down to the coast, where they look for easier means to pay back their debt. For it can be repayed in tokens, which people earn by all the ordinary trades. Some become farmers, some workers, others stevedors, and so on. We have no unkind words for them, for they made it possible for us to buy supplies, rent mules and hire porters.

'And if you don't succeed in paying your debt?' Beaver had asked.

'When you raise chickens,' he was told, 'you give them grain, which they have to pay back in eggs once they become hens. When a pullet doesn't begin laying at the proper age, what becomes of it?'

Each of us swallowed his saliva in silence.

The third day after our arrival, while I was setting down these notes, Judith Pancake was making a few sketches from the doorway, and Sogol was struggling over some difficult optical problems. The five others had gone off in various directions. My wife was shopping for provisions, escorted by Hans and Karl, who, on the way, kept up an obscure dialectical discussion on cruel metaphysical and para-mathematical questions. They were bickering principally over the curvature of time and of numbers: Might there be an absolute limit to any count of real singular objects, after which one would either return abruptly to unity (according to Hans) or reach totality (according to Karl)? Anyway, they arrived home in a very heated state, scarcely noticing the weight of foodstuffs they were carrying on their backs. They brought back vegetables and fruits, some familiar and some unknown to us, for settlers had introduced them from every continent, dairy products, fish, and other foods welcome after a long ocean voyage. The bag of tokens was fat, and we didn't worry much about expenses. And then, as Lapse said, 'Things have to run their own course.'

Lapse had walked around the town chatting with everyone he met in order to study the speech and social life of the place. He gave us an absorbing account, but what happened to us after lunch deprives me of any desire to repeat what he found out. All the same I must. I'm not writing for my own amusement, and some details could be helpful to you at this juncture.

The economic life of Port o' Monkeys is very simple, though animated – very much like it must have been in a little European town before the great mechanical inventions, for no form of engine – steam, gasoline, or other – is admitted into the country. All use of electricity is forbidden, a fact that surprised us in a mountainous land. Explosives are also taboo. The settlement – mostly French, as I have pointed out – has its churches, its municipal council and its own police force. But all authority comes from above – that is, from the high mountain guides – whose delegates administer the town and the constabulary. This authority is unchallenged, for it is based on the possession of peradams. People residing along the coast possess only tokens, which permit all exchanges indispensable for material existence but confer no real power. Let me repeat that we have no criticism to make of any of the people who, discouraged by the hardships of the ascent, have settled on the coast and on the lower slopes and have made a life for themselves there. Thanks to them, thanks to their original effort to reach this land, their children at least have no such voyage to make. They are born on the shores of Mount Analogue, less subject to the harmful influences of degenerate cultures that flourish on our continents, frequently dealing with men from higher up, and able, if the desire possesses them and their intelligence awakens, to undertake the great journey onward from the spot where their parents abandoned it.

The bulk of the town's population, however, appears to have a different origin. They are descendants of the crews, slaves or sailors from ships brought to these parts ever since the remotest times by seekers of the Mountain. This explained the abundance of little-known strains, among which one could identify African and Asiatic types and even races now extinct. Since women must have been rare among these early expeditions, nature's laws of compensation must have reestablished equilibrium between the sexes by a preponderance of female births. In all that I am setting down there are a good many suppositions.

According to accounts given to Lapse by the residents of Port o' Monkeys, life in the other coastal towns is very much the same, with small variations in customs and language introduced by each nation and race. All languages, however, since the immemorial era of the first settlers, have evolved in a particular fashion under the influence of the guides, who have a special language, and in spite of any new contributions made by contemporary settlers. The French spoken in Port o' Monkeys, for example, has a good many peculiarities, with archaisms and borrowed forms along with newly coined words to designate new objects, like 'peradam'. These oddities were to be explained later on as we became more familiar with the language of the guides.

Arthur Beaver, intrigued by the flora and fauna of the region, came back beet-red from a long walk in the nearby countryside. The temperate climate of Port o' Monkeys favours the growth of plants and animals known in our countries, but one also finds unfamiliar species. Several of them are real curiosities: a kind of arborescent bindweed whose powers of germination and growth are so great that it is used – like slow-motion dynamite – to unseat boulders for purposes of building and terracing; the incendiary lycoperdon, like an overgrown puffball, which bursts when ripe, throws its spores a great distance, and spontaneously ignites a few hours later as a result of intense fermentation; the talking bush, a rare and sensitive plant whose fruits grow in the shape of resonant gourds of divers shapes capable of reproducing all the sounds of the human voice when rubbed by its own leaves, a bush that repeats like a parrot any words pronounced near it; the hoop caterpillar, a myriapod about two yards long, which likes to form into a circle and roll headlong from top to bottom of stony slopes; and the cyclops lizard, resembling a chameleon but with a single staring frontal eye, whereas the two others are atrophied, an animal that enjoys considerable respect even though it looks like an aged teacher of heraldry. Among numerous insect species there is the aeronaut grub, something like a silk worm, which in good weather generates light gases in its intestines and in a few hours blows up a huge bubble that carries it off into the atmosphere; it never reaches full maturity and reproduces itself ingloriously by larval parthenogenesis.

Had these curious species been brought in long ago by settlers from other parts of the earth, or were they forms of life truly indigenous to the continent of Mount Analogue? Beaver could not resolve the question. An old Breton, established in Port o' Monkeys as a carpenter, had related and sung to him some old myths that touched on the subject. They were a kind of blend, it seems, of foreign legends and the guides' teachings. Any guides we later asked about the value of these myths always gave us what appeared to be evasive answers. 'They are as true,' one of them told us, 'as your own fairy stories and scientific theories.' 'A knife,' said another, 'is neither true nor false. But someone who grasps it by the blade is truly in error.'

One of the myths went something like this:

In the beginning the Sphere and the Tetrahedron were united in a single inconceivable Form: Concentration and Expansion mysteriously fused in a single Will, which willed only its own being.

There came a separation, but the Unique remains unique.

The Sphere became primordial Man, who, wishing to realize separately all his desires and possibilities, scattered himself into all the animal species and men of today.

The Tetrahedron became the primordial Plant, which likewise engendered all plants.

Animals, closed away from exterior space, hollow themselves out and ramify internally, developing lungs, intestines and other organs to receive nourishment, conserve energy, and sustain life. Plants, spreading out into space, ramify externally in order to penetrate their nourishment with roots and leaves.

A few of their descendants wavered or tried to belong to both camps. They became the animal-plants that populate the seas.

Man received breath and the light of understanding; he alone received this light. He wished to see his light and delight in its changing shapes. He was driven out by the force of the One. He alone was driven out.

He went out then to people the lands Beyond, toiling, dividing against himself, and multiplying in the desire to see his own light and enjoy it.

Sometimes a man humbles himself in his heart, submits the visible to the power to see, and seeks to return to his source.

He seeks, he finds, and he returns to his source.

The curious geological structure of the continent has given it a wide variety of climates, and a three-day journey from Port o'

Monkeys brings you to the jungle in one direction, to glacial terrain in another, elsewhere to steppes or to sandy desert. Each colony had been established in the place that most closely resembled the native land of the settlers.

For Beaver, all that was still to be explored. Karl proposed to study the Asiatic origins he detected in the myths Beaver had collected. On a nearby hill Hans and Sogol hoped to build a little observatory from which, under the peculiar optical conditions of the country, they would perform the standard measurements of parallaxes, angular distances, meridian passages, spectroscopy and the like. They wanted to reach precise conclusions about the anomalies in cosmic perspective caused by the shell of curved space surrounding Mount Analogue. Ivan Lapse planned to continue his linguistic and sociological researches. My wife was eager to study the religious life of the country, the modifications (and above all, she supposed, the purifications and enrichments) introduced into the several sects by the influence of Mount Analogue – changes in dogma, ethics, rites, liturgical music, architecture, and the other religious arts. Miss Pancake would work with her, especially on the plastic arts, while continuing her enormous task of documentary sketching. This had assumed considerable importance for the expedition after the failure of all attempts at photography. For my part, I expected to draw on all the materials gathered by my companions in order to further my investigations in symbolic process and theory, but without neglecting my principal responsibility of keeping the daily journal of the expedition. The journal was later shortened to this account you are reading.

While pursuing these various tasks, we planned to turn them to profit as best we could in order to enlarge our stock of provisions – to transact business if necessary. In short, we should not be wasting our time.

'When are you getting under way?' a voice shouted up from the street one day. We were sitting around after lunch talking excitedly about all our activities.

It was the guide assigned to Port o' Monkeys who had challenged us. Without waiting for an answer, he went on down the street with the steady pace of a mountaineer who looks as if he is barely moving.

That roused us from our dreams. Before having taken even the first steps, we were already slipping towards disaster – yes, towards giving up. For to devote a single minute to satisfying idle curiosity amounted to abandoning our goal and betraying our word. All our enthusiasm for exploration suddenly struck us as trivial, along with the clever pretexts we had found for those pastimes. We barely dared look at one another. Sogol muttered in low, grim tones:

'Let's nail that nasty owl to the door and get out without looking back.'

We all knew only too well that vile creature of intellectual cupidity, and each of us had his own owl to nail to the door along with a few chattering magpies, parading turkey-cocks, cooing doves and geese, lots of fat geese! But all those creatures are so securely anchored, grafted so deeply into our flesh, that we cannot cast them away without tearing out our very insides. We had to go on living with them for a long time, enduring them, coming to know them well, until they fell from us as the scabs of an eruptive disease come off, of themselves, when the system becomes healthy again. It is damaging to rip them off prematurely.

Our four crewmen were playing cards under a pine tree. Since they had no ambition to climb the higher slopes, their way of passing the time appeared entirely reasonable compared to ours. They were to help us with the baggage, however, and we called them to give us a hand preparing for the departure. We resolved to leave the next day, at any cost.

It was easier said than done. The next morning, after we had worked all night making up the packs, everything was ready; the porters and the donkeys were waiting. But it began to rain in torrents. It rained all afternoon; it rained that night; it rained the following day; it rained buckets for five days. We were told that the roads and trails would certainly be washed out.

The delay had to be put to some use. First we made a new inventory of our equipment. All kinds of instruments for observation and measurement, which had seemed the most precious of all before, now seemed ridiculous – especially after our fruitless attempts at photography. Other devices turned out to be quite useless. Since the batteries of our lamps did not work, they would have to be replaced by lanterns. Thus we got rid of a good deal of excess equipment and could take along that many more provisions.

We scoured the neighbourhood to procure further provisions, lanterns and clothing. The clothes made in the town, although very simple in design, were far superior to ours because of the residents' long experience. In certain specialized stores we found all kinds of dried and preserved food; it would be very precious to us. We kept eliminating one thing after another until we ended up leaving behind even Beaver's 'portable gardens'. After a day of grumpy indecision he let out a great whoop of laughter and declared that they were 'stupid playthings which would have given us nothing but bother and indigestion'. He hesitated a little longer over the respiratory apparatus and heated clothing. Finally we decided to leave it all behind, with the possibility of coming back to get it for a later attempt if necessary. We left all these things in the care of the crew, who carried them back to the yacht, where they were to live after our departure. For the house had to be vacated in readiness for new arrivals.

The matter of respiratory equipment was debated heatedly. In order to enter high altitudes, should we rely on bottled oxygen or on our capacity to adapt ourselves? Recent expeditions in the Himalayas had not solved the problem in spite of the brilliant successes of those advocating acclimatization. Furthermore, our equipment was a vast improvement over that employed on those expeditions. Not only was it lighter, but it ought also to be more efficient, since it furnished the climber not with pure oxygen but with a carefully regulated mixture of oxygen and carbon dioxide. The presence of the latter gas, a stimulant to the respiratory centres, should permit a considerable reduction in the amount of oxygen required. But the more we thought it over and the more information we gathered on the nature of the mountains we were approaching, the clearer it became that our expedition would be long, very long. It would certainly last several years. Our oxygen supply would not be sufficient, and we would have no means of recharging the cylinders up above. Sooner or later we would have to give them up, and it would be better to get rid of them right away so as not to delay the process of acclimatization by using them. Moreover, we were assured that the only sure means of survival in the higher altitudes was to become gradually accustomed to the conditions, and that the human organism can adapt itself far more radically than we might have suspected.

On the advice of the head porter we exchanged our skis, which would have hampered us on many steep and narrow trails, for narrow collapsible snow-shoes stretched with marmot skin, which not only make it easier to walk in deep snow but can be used also in sliding down slopes for a fast descent. Folded up, they stow away easily in a pack. We wore hob-nailed boots for the time being, but we took along to wear later moccasins made locally out of 'tree leather', a sort of bark that resembles both leather and cork when properly treated. This material insulates very well and, with fragments of silica embedded in it, adheres to ice almost as well as to stone. These shoes would enable us to dispense with spikes, which are dangerous at high altitudes because the straps bind the feet, reduce circulation, and increase the chances of frostbite. On the other hand, we kept our pistols, superb weapons that could scarcely be improved on any more than a scythe. And we kept our picks, silk ropes and, in spite of all, a few simple pocket instruments like compasses, altimeters and thermometers.

We ended up by being thankful for the rain, which allowed us to make so many advantageous changes in our gear. Every day we walked a great deal through the downpour, seeking information and supplies, and thanks to that, our legs, weakened and stiffened by the long voyage, grew strong again.

It was during these rainy days that we began to call one another by our first names. The ground had already been prepared by the habit we had of saying 'Hans' and 'Karl', but the change was not the effect of mere intimacy. We now called one another Judith, Renée (my wife's name), Pierre, Arthur, Ivan, Theodore (my name) out of a new sense of things which affected each of us. For we were beginning to shed our old personalities. At the same time as we decided to leave our heavy equipment on the coast, we were also preparing to leave behind the artist, the inventor, the doctor, the scholar, the writer. Beneath the old disguises new men and new women began to show the tips of their ears. Men and women, and all kinds of other creatures as well.

Once again Pierre Sogol set an example – without knowing it and without suspecting that the poet in him was coming out. One evening when we had just finished a consultation on the beach with the head porter and the donkey driver, Sogol began to speak.

'I have brought you this far, and I have been your leader. Right here I'll take off the cap of authority, which was a crown of thorns for the person I remember myself to be. Far within me, where the memory of what I am still is unclouded, a little child is waking up and making an old man's mask weep. A little child looking for mother and father, looking with you for protection and help – protection from his pleasures and his dreams, and help in order to become what he is without imitating anyone.'

As he spoke, Pierre had been delving in the sand with the point of his stick. Suddenly his eyes froze; he bent down and picked something up – something that shone like a tiny dewdrop. It was a peradam, a small one, but the first for any of us.

The head porter and the donkey driver turned pale, and their eyes widened. Both were old men who had attempted the ascent and had lost heart out of lack of resources.

'Never,' the porter said, 'never in anyone's memory was one ever found so far down. Right on the beach! Perhaps it's just luck. But could it be a sign of new hope for us? Is it time to set out once again?'

A hope, which he thought long dead, glowed again in his heart. That man would try again one day. The mule driver's eyes shone too – but out of envy.

'Luck, sheer luck: I won't let myself be caught again.'

And Judith Pancake said, 'We'll all have to make little sachets to wear around our necks for the peradams we find.'

It was an indispensable precaution. The rain had stopped the previous day, and the sun had begun to dry the trails. We were to set out at dawn the following day. As a last preparation each of us, before going to bed, carefully made a little sack for future peradams.

5

Which Is That of Setting Up the First Camp

The chalet at the base – Our welcome at the second camp – The trail keeps changing – Sending supplies to the preceding caravan – Hunting (prohibited higher up: biological equilibrium) – The story of the head porter – The other expedition, like our shadow before us – The disappearance of the Diane *– Advice from the guides: an old story but a new meaning – The 'uncurving lens' – Observations . . .*

Darkness still drifted around us under the fir trees, whose tops etched their fine writing against an already luminous sky. Then, lower down on the trunks, red tints appeared, and several of us saw the sky slowly open to show the pure washed blue of our grandmothers' eyes. Little by little the full spectrum of greens emerged out of the black, and every so often the fragrance of a beech freshened the smell of resin and contrasted with the scent of mushrooms. With voices like rattles or burbling springs or tinkling silver or flutes, the birds exchanged their morning small talk. We walked in silence. With ten mules, fifteen porters, and the three crewmen in the lead, our caravan was fairly long. Each of us carried his ration of provisions for the day and his personal effects. Several of us had some pretty weighty personal effects to carry in our hearts and minds as well. We quickly fell into the mountaineer's steady pack-carrying stride, a rhythm it is wise to adopt from the beginning if one wants to keep going for a long time without fatigue. While walking, I went over in my mind the series of events which had brought me so far – from my article in the *Revue des Fossiles* and the meeting with Sogol down to the present. Fortunately the donkeys were trained not to walk too fast; they reminded me of those I had known in Bigorre, and I found strength in looking at the supple flow of their muscles unbroken by useless contractions. I thought of the four who had dropped out with their lame excuses. How far away they all were, Julie Bonasse and Emile Gorge and Cicoria and old Alphonse Camard with his wayfaring songs. It seemed another world already. I began to laugh to myself at the memory of those songs. As if mountain climbers ever sing while they walk! Sure, you sing once in a while after scrambling a few hours over rubble or tramping in the grass. But it's each man for himself, and probably between clenched teeth. For example, my song goes like this: 'Tyak, tyak, tyak.' One 'tyak' for every step. In snow and around noontime it becomes 'Tyak, chee chee, tyak.' Someone else may sing: 'Stoom, dee dee, stoom' or 'Gee . . . pouf. Gee . . . pouf.' That's the only kind of mountain-climbing song I know.

We were no longer in sight of the snow-covered summits but only of wooded slopes cut by limestone cliffs, and down vistas through the forest to the right, the torrent at the bottom of the valley. At the last turn in the path the ocean, whose horizon had continued to rise with us, had gone out of sight. I nibbled a piece of biscuit. A donkey kept fanning a cloud of flies into my face with its tail. My companions were as pensive as I was. After all, there was something mysterious about the ease with which we had landed on the continent of Mount Analogue; it still seemed certain that we had been expected. I imagined it would all be explained in due time. Bernard, the head porter, was absorbed in his own thoughts like the rest of us, but not so distracted. For our attention was constantly being caught by a blue squirrel or by a red-eyed ermine standing erect like a column in the middle of an emerald clearing spattered with orange agaric or by a herd of unicorns which we had first taken for chamois and which went leaping across a bare outcropping on the opposite slope or by a flying lizard that sped ahead of us from one tree to the next, snapping its jaws. Except for Bernard, all the porters carried on their packs a little bow of horn and a bundle of stubby featherless arrows. At the first major halt, a little before noon, three or four of the men went off and came back with some pheasants and a sort of oversized guinea pig. One of them said to me, 'You have to take advantage of the game while you can. We'll eat these tonight. Higher up, there's no hunting.'

The path came out of the forest and wound down through bright sunny clearings to the mountain torrent, which muttered and chuckled like an animated crowd. We crossed by a ford, stirring up clouds of iridescent butterflies from the damp bank, and crossed a wide stony area without any shade. When we veered back to the right bank, an airy forest of larches began. I was sweating and singing my little song. Though we appeared more and more thoughtful all the time, actually we were much less so now. The trail climbed up over a high rocky promontory and turned to the right, where the valley narrowed into a deep gorge; then the trail twisted pitilessly upward back and forth across a steep scrub of junipers and rhododendrons. We finally came out in a high pasture watered by countless little brooks, where some tubby cows were quietly grazing. Twenty minutes of walking through the soaking grass brought us to a small pebbly plateau, shaded by larches. There we found several stone buildings crudely covered with branches; it was our first night's stopping-place. We still had two or three hours of daylight during which to settle in. One of the shelters was for the baggage; another served as sleeping quarters, with boards, clean straw, and a stone fireplace for cooking. To our surprise the third building was equipped as a dairy; jugs of milk, chunks of butter and dripping cheeses were stored there, as if in expectation of our arrival. Was the place lived in? Bernard, whose first act was to order his men to stack their bows and arrows in a corner of the shelter along with the slings a few of them carried, gave us the explanation.

'It was lived in right up to this morning. There always has to be someone here to take care of the cows. It's a regulation they'll explain to you higher up; no encampment can ever remain unoccupied more than one day. The preceding caravan probably left a couple of men here and is waiting up ahead for us to arrive before going on. From here the men could see us coming and must have left right away. We'll let them know we've arrived, and at the same time I can show you where the base trail starts.'

We followed him a little way along a rocky ledge to a platform from which we could see the head of the valley. It was formed like a circus in an irregular closed oval, broken only by the gorge where we stood and surrounded by steep slopes rising towards the summit, from which the huge tongue of a glacier hung down here and there. Bernard lit a fire, threw some moist grass on it, and looked towards the head of the valley. After a few minutes we saw in the distance an answering signal go up, a thin thread of white smoke hard to distinguish from the slow mist of the waterfalls.

In the mountains a man becomes very attentive to any sign indicating the presence of one of his fellow men. That distant smoke was particularly moving for us, a greeting sent us by strangers climbing ahead of us on the same trail. For from now on the trail linked our fate to theirs, even if we were never to meet. Bernard knew nothing about them.

From where we stood we could see about half of the second day's journey. We had decided to take advantage of the good weather and leave the following morning. We might have the good luck to find our guide at the base the same day, but we might have to wait for him to come back from a short or even a long trip. The eight of us would set out the next day with all the porters except two, who would stay behind to tend the cows. The donkeys and their drivers would climb down again and pick up another load of our equipment. We calculated that in eight trips they could transport all our clothing and provisions from the coast to Meadowbrook, the name of that first encampment. During that time we would shuttle back and forth with the porters between Meadowbrook and the base. It would take us something like thirty trips, with packs of twenty-five to thirty-five pounds. Allowing for bad weather, we would then have stored at the base enough to live on for two years or more. But it meant two months in the cow pastures! The younger ones among us were a little impatient at the prospect.

We could hardly talk up there on the platform because of a high thundering waterfall a few hundred yards away. A footbridge, if you could call it that, consisting of three or four cables strung from one bank to the other, crossed the gorge into which the water fell. The next morning we would have to go over it. Just this side of the waterfall stood a sort of large cairn with a cross on top – a calvary or a burial mound. Benard looked at it with a strange seriousness, then shook off his preoccupation and took us back to the shelter, where the porters had prepared the meal. Thanks to their resourcefulness, we scarcely had to fall back on our supplies. Along the way they had gathered some excellent mushrooms and thistle buds, all of them tasty either raw or boiled. The game was relished by everyone except Bernard, who wouldn't touch it. We noticed he made sure that no one had touched the bows and other arms since our arrival. But it was only after the meal, after the setting sun had lit the wooded slopes from below with vivid colour, while we were sitting quietly around the fire and began to put a few questions to him about the monument next to the waterfall – only then did Bernard begin to open up a little.

'That's my brother,' he said briefly. 'I'd better tell you the whole story, because we may be together for a while and you should know what kind of a man [he spat in the fire] you're dealing with.

'My men act like babies, complaining about the hunting regulations from here on up. There's lots of good game everywhere, I'm not denying. But the guides up above know what they're doing when they forbid hunting beyond Meadowbrook. They have reasons, and I have cause to know. For a rat I killed fifty paces from here I lost the four peradams I'd gone through hell to find and hold on to. And I lost ten years of my life as well . . .

'I come from a peasant family which has lived for centuries in Port o' Monkeys. Several of my ancestors left for the mountain and became guides. But my parents, fearing that I, their eldest son, would leave too, did everything they could to protect me from the call of the mountain. With this in mind, they urged me to marry very young. Down below I have a wife I love and a grown son. He could try the ascent now if he wanted, and so could she. After my parents' death when I was thirty-five, I suddenly saw the emptiness of my life. What was I doing? Was I to go on bringing up my son so that he in turn could carry on the line, and so on? What for? I'm not very good at expressing myself, as you see, and I was worse off then. The whole business seemed to strangle me. One day a guide of the upper mountains who was going through Port o' Monkeys came in to buy provisions from me. I went for him, shook him by the shoulders with nothing better to shout at him but "Why? Why?"

'He answered me gravely, "It's true. But you must begin to think of *how.*" He talked to me for a long time, that day and the days that followed. Finally we arranged to meet the next spring – it was autumn at the time – at the base chalets. He accepted me as one of a caravan he would be forming then. I persuaded my brother to come with me. He too wanted to know why and to free himself from the stifling atmosphere of the coastal area.

'Our expedition of twelve reached the first camp in time to winter there. In the spring I decided to go back down to Port o' Monkeys to see my wife and son in the hope of persuading them to accompany me. Between the base chalets and this camp where we are now I was caught in a very bad blizzard lasting three days. The trail was buried in twenty places by avalanches. For two nights running I had to bivouac with insufficient rations and without fuel. When the weather cleared, I was a hundred yards from here. Exhausted and famished, I stopped to camp. At that time the cattle had not yet been brought up to Meadowbrook, and I found nothing to eat. Then on the slope right opposite me I saw an old rock rat come out of his hole. It's something between a field mouse and a groundhog. It came out to warm itself in the sun. Picking up a stone, I smashed its skull with a lucky throw, cooked it over a fire of rhododendrons, and devoured the leathery meat. Then I slept an hour or two and went on down to

Port o' Monkeys, where my wife and son and I celebrated our reunion after so long a separation. However, I could not persuade them to come back up with me that year . . .

'A month later, as I was about to start up the mountain again, I was called before the guides' tribunal to answer for the murder of the rat. How they learned about it I'll never know. The law makes no exceptions. Access to the mountain above Meadowbrook was denied me for three years. After that I could ask to leave with the first caravan on the condition that I make reparations for any damage my action might have caused. It was a numbing blow. I forced myself to set up again in Port o' Monkeys. With my brother and my son, I farmed and raised cattle to provide supplies for the caravans. We organized teams of porters and hired out their services as far as the prohibited zone. That way, while earning a living, we kept in touch with the mountain people. Before long my brother also was bitten by the desire to leave, by that need for the higher regions which gets into your system like a poison. But he decided he would not leave without me and wanted to wait for the expiration of my punishment.

'Finally the day arrived. I proudly carried with me in a cage a fat rock rat which I had captured easily and which I would free as we went by the place where I had killed the other one – for I had to repair the damage. Alas, the damage had just begun to show. As we left Meadowbrook just at sunrise, a terrifying sound filled the valley. The entire side of the mountain, which was not then cut through by the waterfall, collapsed and crashed down in an avalanche of rocks and mud. A cataract of water, mixed with blocks of ice and stone, burst out of the tip of the glacier, which hung down to the upper slope, and wore great gulleys in the sides of the mountain. The trail, which at that time climbed after leaving Meadowbrook to cross the slope much higher up, was obliterated for a considerable distance. For several days rock slides and eruptions of water and mud kept occurring, and our path was completely blocked. The caravan went back down to Port o' Monkeys in order to re-equip for unforeseen dangers and then set out in search of a new trail to the base chalets along the other bank – a long, mean trail on which several men perished. I was not allowed to leave until a commission of guides had determined the causes of the catastrophe. A week later I was called before the commission, which declared that I was responsible for the disaster, and following the original sentence, would have to repair the damage.

'I was dumbfounded. But they explained to me how it had all happened, according to the findings of the commission. They made the statement impartially, objectively, and today I would even say leniently, but categorically. The old rat I had killed fed principally on a species of wasp common in that spot. But beyond a certain age a rock rat is no longer agile enough to catch wasps on the wing. Therefore he lived for the most part on the sick or weak insects which dragged themselves along the ground and could barely fly. In this way he destroyed the wasps that were malformed or carriers of disease. His unsuspecting intervention protected the colonies of these insects from dangerous afflictions spread by heredity or contagion. Once the rat was dead, these afflictions spread rapidly, and by the following spring there was scarcely a wasp left in the region. These wasps, visiting flowers in search of honey, also fertilized them. Without the wasps, a large number of plants which play an important part in holding the terrain in place,

Postface

Thus, René Daumal stopped in the middle of a sentence in the fifth chapter of *Mount Analogue*. His politeness would not allow him to keep the visitor waiting who knocked on his door that day in April 1944. It was the last on which he held a pen.

His intimate friend, A. Rolland de Renéville, who could not help knowing that Daumal did not have long to live, had the idea of asking him to outline the rest of the novel. Renéville said that his wife, Cassilda, who had read all the text as far as it went, could not wait to know how it ended. With his customary blend of gravity and humour, René Daumal produced a summary of what was to come:

'In the fifth and sixth chapters I plan to describe the expedition of the four quitters. You remember that at the start there were four other characters: Julie Bonasse, a Belgian actress, Benito Cicoria, a woman's tailor, Emile Gorge, a journalist, and Alphonse Camard, a prolific poet – all of whom backed out before we really got under way. In the end, however, along with a few friends, they decided to set out on their own to discover Mount Analogue, for they were convinced that we had hoodwinked them: if we were out to discover this famous mountain, it was not a superior race of humanity we were after. That's why they called us jokers. They thought that the mountain must be sitting on top of oil or gold or some other treasure and must be jealously guarded by a people who would have to be subdued. As a result they fitted out a veritable warship with the most powerful and modern equipment they could find and weighed anchor. Their voyage took them through a series of adventures, and when they finally arrived within sight of Mount Analogue, they prepared to unlimber all their firepower. However, since they were completely ignorant of the laws of the place, they were caught in a whirlpool. Condemned to turn round and round in slow circles, they could still bombard the coast, but all their shells came back at them like boomerangs. It was a ludicrous fate.

'At the end I want to speak at length of one of the basic laws of Mount Analogue. To reach the summit, one must proceed from encampment to encampment. But before setting out for the next refuge, one must prepare those coming after to occupy the place one is leaving. Only after having prepared them can one go on up. That is why, before setting out for a new refuge, we had to go back down* in order to pass on our knowledge to other seekers . . .'

Probably René Daumal would have made clear what he meant by this work of preparation. For in his daily life he devoted himself to preparing many minds for the difficult voyage towards Mount Analogue.

The title of his last chapter was to be:

And you, what do you seek?

It is a more disturbing and fruitful question than the numerous stock answers made to it, a question each of us must finally answer to himself. To face it directly is to strike against the deepest layer of being which sleeps within us, and then one must listen painfully and lucidly to the sound it sends back.

At the end of his short life, though only on the threshold of his own search, René Daumal could already distinguish what is hollow from what is sound and whole. And it is just because his work was interrupted that we should like to understand it better and to know in what direction he was moving.

* '. . . *nous avons dû redescendre* . . .' This could also be rendered: 'we have had to come back down.' The latter reading identifies Daumal's own text as a means of preparing others. [Translator's note.]

On one occasion he did describe in concise terms the path he saw before him. The text appears in one of the last letters he wrote me:

This is how I sum up for myself what I wish to convey to those who work here with me:

> *I am dead because I lack desire;*
> *I lack desire because I think I possess;*
> *I think I possess because I do not try to give.*
> *In trying to give, you see that you have nothing;*
> *Seeing you have nothing, you try to give of yourself;*
> *Trying to give of yourself, you see that you* are *nothing;*
> *Seeing you are nothing, you desire to become;*
> *In desiring to become, you begin to live.*

VÉRA DAUMAL

Editor's Note

According to René Daumal's last working notes, *Mount Analogue* was to have been made up of seven chapters. Instead of reconstituting the missing part of the narrative, we have decided to publish two key outlines.

The first concerns Chapter 5. It gives us a glimpse of what happened to Bernard, the head porter, and mentions the two remaining themes: 'sending supplies to the preceding group' and 'the guides' language'.

The second document (given in facsimile only) sketches in Chapter 6 – it would have told about 'the other expedition' of Alphonse Camard, Emile Gorge, Julie Bonasse and Benito Cicoria (see pages 63–4) which could only end in catastrophe – and 7, in which Daumal would probably have addressed the reader directly.

Between 1938 and 1942, René Daumal wrote several other texts very important for understanding *Mount Analogue*. We give them here in chronological order.

The first is the opening of 'Treatise on Analogical Mountain Climbing', conceived well before the composition of *Mount Analogue*. The second is made up of two introductory paragraphs which, instead of summarizing the opening, simply allow the reader to enter the story, and of two paragraphs which reveal how Daumal planned 'to clothe this veracious story in order to make it believable'. These paragraphs framed Chapter 1 as it appeared in the review *Mésures* (No. 1, January 1940).

good-byes
to the crew
the sea's horizon behind us
showed – the dawn

---

while walking . . .
reflections (mystery of so easy an arrival)
songs (tyak! tyak!)

cabins at the base
setting up the first camp
first exercises
guides' advice
accident

overnight stop
at the first refuge

ermine
unicorns

hunting (prohibited higher up: ecological balance)
head porter's story (hunts – has to pay back – gets discouraged)
hunted for 3 years

Base Camp
rat
bees
plants
landslides
rocks
ice pocket . . .

bridge

?*cards*?

need to send supplies to the preceding group
?homing pigeons?

the sun burns!
– 'clouds'
guides' language

V –

conseils des guides : connus, mais sens nouveau

... du 1er camp ...

guides – degrés : 7 ou 49 ou 8 ou 10 ou 5C ..
(nombres...)
nombres = degrés.

Langue.

invités au 2e camp, par petits groupes, par le guide n° 2 – de là, par la "lunette déconcertante", observons...

VI – L'autre expédition

récit de Julie Bonasse, rescapée (?)

Le Petit Informé

VII

" et vous alors ? "
que cherchez-vous ?

1

Foreword – These are the observations of a beginner. Since they are still fresh in my mind and deal with elementary difficulties, a beginner doing his first climbs may find them more useful than systematic treatises for advanced climbers. The single intention of these notes is to help the beginner to acquire his initial experience a little faster.

Definitions. – *Alpinism* is the art of climbing mountains in such a way as to face the greatest risks with the greatest prudence.

Art is here taken to mean knowledge realized in action.

You cannot stay on the summit forever; you have to come down again . . . So why bother in the first place? Just this: What is above knows what is below, but what is below does not know what is above. In climbing, take careful note of the difficulties along your way; for as you go up, you can observe them. Coming down, you will no longer see them, but you will know they are there if you have observed them well.

There is an art of finding one's direction in the lower regions by the memory of what one saw higher up. When one can no longer see, one can at least still know.

I asked him, 'What do you mean by "analogical mountain climbing"?'
– It's the art of . . .
– What is an art?
– The value of danger:
  temerity → suicide
  Short of it, no satisfaction.

– What is danger?
– What is prudence?
– What is a mountain?

Keep your eye fixed on the way to the top, but don't forget to look right in front of you. The last step depends on the first. Don't think you've arrived just because you see the summit. Watch your footing, be sure of the next step, but don't let that distract you from the *highest goal.* The first step depends on the last.

When you strike off on your own, leave some trace of your passing which will guide you coming back: one stone set on another, some grass flattened by a blow of your stick. But if you come to an impasse or a dangerous spot, remember that the trail you have left could lead people coming after you into trouble. So go back along your trial and obliterate any traces you have left. This applies to anyone who wishes to leave some mark of his passage in the world. Even without wanting to, you always leave a few traces. Be ready to answer to your fellow men for the trail you leave behind you.

Never halt on a shifting slope. Even if you think you have a firm foothold, as you take time to catch your breath and have a look at the sky, the ground will settle little by little under your weight, the gravel will begin to slip imperceptibly, and suddenly it will drop away under you and launch you like a ship. The mountain is always watching for a chance to give you a spill.

If, after climbing up and down three steep gulleys that end in a sheer wall (visible only at the last minute), your legs begin to tremble and your teeth to chatter, head for the nearest ledge where you can rest securely. Then rack your brain for all the oaths you have ever heard and hurl them at the mountain, spit on it, insult it as violently as you know how. Take a swallow of water, have a bite to eat, and then start climbing again, easily, slowly, as if you had a lifetime ahead of you in which to pull out of the bad spot. That night before falling asleep, when this comes back to you, you'll see how much of an act you were putting on: you weren't talking to the mountain at all, nor was it the mountain you got the better of. The mountain is nothing but rock and ice, with neither ears nor heart. But that little act may have saved your life.

Besides, often at difficult moments you'll catch yourself talking to the mountain, flattering it, cursing it, making promises or threats. And you will have the impression that the mountain answers you if you speak to it properly – by becoming gentler, more submissive. Don't think the less of yourself for that; don't be ashamed of behaving like those our specialists call primitives and animists. Just keep in mind, when you remember these moments later on, that your dialogue with nature was just the outward image of an inner dialogue with yourself.

Shoes, unlike feet, are not something you're born with. So you can choose what you want. At first be guided in your choice by people with experience, later by your own experience. Before long you will become so accustomed to your shoes that every nail will be like a finger to feel out the rock and cling to it. They will become a sensitive and dependable instrument, like a part of yourself. And yet, you're not born with them; when they're worn out, you'll throw them away and still remain what you are.

Your life depends to some extent on your shoes; care for them properly. But a quarter of an hour each day is enough, for your life depends on several other things as well.

A fellow climber with far more experience than I has told me: 'When your feet will no longer carry you, you have to walk with your head.' And it's true. Perhaps it's not in the natural order of things, but isn't it better to walk with your head than to think with your feet; as happens only too often?

If you slip or have a minor fall, don't allow yourself an instant's pause. Find your pace again the moment you get up. In your mind take careful note of the circumstances of your fall, but don't let your body linger over what happened. The body constantly tries to draw attention to itself by its shiverings, its breathlessness, its palpitations, its shudders and sweats and cramps; but it reacts quickly to any scorn and indifference in its master. Once it senses that he is not taken in by its jeremiads, once it understands that it will inspire no pity for itself that way, then it comes into line and obediently accomplishes its task.

The moment of danger
The difference between panic and presence of mind
Automatism (master or servant)

2

I would have preferred to tell you the whole story right now. Since that would take too long, here is the beginning. Possibly it is deceptive to speak of the beginning and end of a story when we never grasp anything but the middle portions. At the heart of the events was an encounter, however, and every encounter is a relative beginning, and this encounter, especially, contains a whole story in itself.

What I have to tell is so unusual that I must take certain precautions. To teach anatomy, conventional diagrams rather than photographs are used, and from every point of view these diagrams are different from the object of study, except that certain relationships – precisely those forming the *thing to be known* – are preserved. I have done the same thing here.

This is the origin of the plan for an expedition to Mount Analogue. Having begun, I must tell what happened: how it was proved that an unknown continent, with mountains as high as the Himalayas, existed on Earth; how it had gone so long unnoticed; how we reached it; what beings we found there; how another expedition, with quite different goals, almost perished in the most frightful way; how we have gradually taken root, so to speak, in this new world; and how, nevertheless, the voyage has barely begun . . .

High up and far off in the sky, above and beyond all the successive circles of rising crests and whitening snows, in a dazzling brilliance the eye cannot bear, made invisible by excess of light, Mount Analogue lifts its ultimate peak. 'There, on a summit as pointed as a needle, broods the solitary being that occupies all space. Up there, in the rarefied air where everything freezes, subsists the crystal of ultimate stability. Up there, unprotected from the sky where everything burns, subsists the perpetual incandescence. There, at the still centre resides the Being who beholds each thing accomplished in its beginning and in its end.' That's what the mountaineers sing here. That's the way it is. 'You say that's the way it is. But if it turns a bit cold, your head feels like a mole's. If it gets hot, your head becomes a swarm of flies. If you get hungry, your body turns into a donkey that won't respond to the stick. If you're tired, your feet defy you.' That's another song the mountaineers are singing now, as I search for a way to clothe this veracious story in order to make it believable.

3

All sorts of voices could be heard. You singled out a few to listen to. One voice told about the man who, coming down from the summits to the lowlands, finds that he can see only his immediate surroundings. 'But he remembers what he has seen and it can still guide him. When you can no longer see, you can still know, and you can testify to what you have seen.' Another voice spoke about shoes, and told how every nail, every scoring on the sole becomes as sensitive as a finger searching the ground for a rough place to hold on to. 'Still, they're merely shoes, you're not born with them, and fifteen minutes of care every day will keep them in good shape. Whereas you're born with your feet, and you'll die with them – at least you expect to. But can you be sure? Aren't there feet that survive their owner? or die before him? (I silenced that voice, it was getting too eschatological.) Another talked about Olympus and Golgotha, another about polyglobulin and the particularities of mountaineers' metabolism. Another insisted that we were 'all wrong in supposing that high mountains have few legends'; it knew at least one remarkable one. It explained that in this legend the mountain served more as setting than as symbol and that the true location of the story was 'at the junction between our humanity and a higher civilization, a place where a superior truth is perpetuated'. Intrigued, I have tried to reproduce the legend as faithfully as I can – which means that you will find here only a faint approximation of it.

4

One August day I was coming down from the hard, bitter region of whiteness, where gusts of sleet were swirling and storms were building up. I knew that all too soon various things would keep me from returning to that celestial country of jagged ridges dancing in the open sky; to the illusion of high and low places in the white cornices that were etched against the blue-black abyss overhead and slowly crumbled in the mid-afternoon silence; and to the slopes carved with ridges and glistening with ice where grapeshot suddenly explodes with the smell of sulphur. Once again I had wanted to sniff the greenish breath of a crevasse, explore a boulder's surface, slip between crumbling rocks, secure a rope, test the rise and fall of an uncertain wind, listen to the sound of steel on ice and the little crystalline clumps tumbling towards the pitfall of a hidden crevasse – a death trap powdered and draped with gems. I wanted to make a track in the diamonds and the flour, entrust myself to two strands of hemp, and eat prunes in the centre of space. Climbing down through a blanket of clouds, I had stopped level with the first saxifrage before a huge ice slide, a gigantic scarf with pearly folds that spiralled downward to the great desert of stones at the bottom.

Then I had to stay below for a long time, resting in bed or gathering flowers, my ice pick put away in the closet. At that point I remembered that I was by profession a writer, and that I had a beautiful opportunity to employ this profession for its usual purpose, which is to speak instead of act. Unable to course through the mountains, I would sing their praises from below. I must admit that I had this intention, but luckily, it gave off a repulsive smell within me, the odour of literature as a stop-gap, of words piled one upon the other to avoid taking action or to console oneself for being incapable of it.

I began to think more seriously, experiencing the heaviness and clumsiness with which thought moves when one has conquered the body by conquering the rocks and ice. I would not speak *of* the mountain but *through* the mountain. With this mountain as a language, I would speak of another mountain that is the path uniting Earth and Heaven, and I would speak of it not to resign myself but to urge myself on. And the whole story – my story up to this point, clothed in the words of the mountain – was laid out before me. A whole story, which I now must have time to tell; and I shall also need time to live it to the end.*

With a group of friends I set out in search of the Mountain which is the path uniting Earth with Heaven and which *must* exist somewhere on our planet and must be the abode of a superior humanity; this was proved to our reason by the man we shall call Father Sogol, the most experienced of us in things of the mountain and the leader of the expedition.

And now we have landed on the unknown continent, this kernel of higher substances implanted in the earth's crust, protected from the eyes of the curious and the greedy by the curvature of its space – like a drop of mercury, impenetrable by virtue of its surface tension to the finger that seeks its centre.

By our calculations, thinking of nothing else, by our desires, abandoning every other hope, by our efforts, renouncing all bodily comfort, we gained entry into this new world. So it seemed to us. But we learned later that if we were able to reach the foot of Mount Analogue, it was because the invisible doors of that invisible country had been opened for us by those who guard them. The cock crowing in the milky dawn thinks its call raises the sun; the child

* This story is the subject of a book in preparation, *Mount Analogue*, which will also incorporate the pages that follow [Daumal's note].

howling in a closed room thinks its cries open the door. But the sun and the mother go their way, following the laws of their beings. Those who see us, even though we cannot see ourselves, opened the door for us, answering our puerile calculations, our unsteady desires and our awkward efforts with a generous welcome.